Enrichment Masters

Glencoe
Algebra
Concepts and Applications

Glencoe
McGraw-Hill

New York, New York   Columbus, Ohio   Woodland Hills, California   Peoria, Illinois

Glencoe/McGraw-Hill

A Division of The McGraw·Hill Companies

Send all inquiries to:
The McGraw-Hill Companies
8787 Orion Place
Columbus, OH 43240-4027

ISBN: 0-07-821944-2

*Algebra
Enrichment Masters*

1 2 3 4 5 6 7 8 9 10   024   07 06 05 04 03 02 01 00

CONTENTS

1-1

Enrichment

Perfect, Excessive, Defective, and Amicable Numbers

A **perfect number** is the sum of all of its factors except itself.
Here is an example.

$$28 = 1 + 2 + 4 + 7 + 14$$

There are very few perfect numbers. Most numbers are either
defective or *excessive*.

An **excessive number** is greater than the sum of all of its
factors except itself.

A **defective number** is less than this sum.

Two numbers are **amicable** if the sum of the factors of the first
number, except for the number itself, equals the second number,
and vice versa.

Solve each problem.

1. Write the perfect numbers between 0 and 31.

2. Write the excessive numbers between 0 and 31.

3. Write the defective numbers between 0 and 31.

4. Show that 8128 is a perfect number.

5. The sum of the reciprocals of all the factors of a perfect
   number (including the number itself) equals 2. Show that
   this is true for the first two perfect numbers.

6. More than 1000 pairs of amicable numbers have been found.
   One member of the first pair is 220. Find the other member.

7. One member of the second pair of amicable numbers is 2620.
   Find the other member.

8. The Greek mathematician Euclid proved that the expression
   $2^{n-1}(2^n - 1)$ equals a perfect number if the expression inside
   the parentheses is prime. Use Euclid's expression with n
   equal to 19 to find the seventh perfect number.

1-1

Enrichment

Perfect, Excessive, Defective, and Amicable Numbers

A **perfect number** is the sum of all of its factors except itself. Here is an example.

$$28 = 1 + 2 + 4 + 7 + 14$$

There are very few perfect numbers. Most numbers are either *defective* or *excessive*.

An **excessive number** is greater than the sum of all of its factors except itself.

A **defective number** is less than this sum.

Two numbers are **amicable** if the sum of the factors of the first number, except for the number itself, equals the second number, and vice versa.

Solve each problem.

1. Write the perfect numbers between 0 and 31.
   6, 28

2. Write the excessive numbers between 0 and 31. **2, 3, 4, 5, 7, 8, 9, 10, 11, 13, 14, 15, 16, 17, 19, 21, 22, 23, 25, 26, 27, 29**

3. Write the defective numbers between 0 and 31.
   12, 18, 20, 24, 30

4. Show that 8128 is a perfect number. **8128 = 1 + 2 + 4 + 8 + 16 + 32 + 64 + 127 + 254 + 508 + 1016 + 2032 + 4064**

5. The sum of the reciprocals of all the factors of a perfect number (including the number itself) equals 2. Show that this is true for the first two perfect numbers.
   $\frac{1}{1} + \frac{1}{2} + \frac{1}{3} + \frac{1}{6} = \frac{12}{6} = 2$ $\frac{1}{1} + \frac{1}{2} + \frac{1}{4} + \frac{1}{7} + \frac{1}{14} + \frac{1}{28} = \frac{56}{28} = 2$

6. More than 1000 pairs of amicable numbers have been found. One member of the first pair is 220. Find the other member.
   284

7. One member of the second pair of amicable numbers is 2620. Find the other member.
   2924

8. The Greek mathematician Euclid proved that the expression $2^{n-1}(2^n - 1)$ equals a perfect number if the expression inside the parentheses is prime. Use Euclid's expression with n equal to 19 to find the seventh perfect number.
   $2^{18}(2^{19} - 1) = 137,438,691,32$

Symmetric, Reflexive, and Transitive Properties

Equality has three important properties.

> Reflexive $a = a$
> Symmetric   If $a = b$, then $b = a$.
> Transitive   If $a = b$ and $b = c$, then $a = c$.

Other relations have some of the same properties. Consider the relation "is next to" for objects labeled X, Y, and Z. Which of the properties listed above are true for this relation?

> X is next to X.   *False*
> If X is next to Y, then Y is next to X.   *True*
> If X is next to Y and Y is next to Z, then X is next to Z.   *False*

Only the Reflexive Property is true for the relation "is next to."

For each relation, state which properties (Symmetric, Reflexive, Transitive) are true.

1. is the same size as

2. is a family descendant of

3. is in the same room as

4. is the identical twin of

5. is warmer than

6. is on the same line as

7. is a sister of

8. is the same weight as

9. Find two other examples of relations, and tell which properties are true for each relation.

1-2 Enrichment

Symmetric, Reflexive, and Transitive Properties

Equality has three important properties.

Reflexive $a = a$
Symmetric   If $a = b$, then $b = a$.
Transitive   If $a = b$ and $b = c$, then $a = c$.

Other relations have some of the same properties. Consider the relation "is next to" for objects labeled X, Y, and Z. Which of the properties listed above are true for this relation?

X is next to X.   *False*
If X is next to Y, then Y is next to X.   *True*
If X is next to Y and Y is next to Z, then X is next to Z.   *False*

Only the Reflexive Property is true for the relation "is next to."

For each relation, state which properties (Symmetric, Reflexive, Transitive) are true.

1. is the same size as
Symmetric, Reflexive, Transitive

2. is a family descendant of
Transitive

3. is in the same room as
Symmetric, Reflexive, transitive

4. is the identical twin of
Symmetric

5. is warmer than
Transitive

6. is on the same line as
Symmetric, Reflexive

7. is a sister of
none

8. is the same weight as
Symmetric, Reflexive Transitive

9. Find two other examples of relations, and tell which properties are true for each relation. **See students' work.**

Enrichment

Valid and Faulty Arguments

Consider the statements at the right. What conclusions can you make?

(1) Boots is a cat.
(2) Boots is purring.
(3) A cat purrs if it is happy.

From statements 1 and 3, it is correct to conclude that Boots purrs if it is happy. However, it is faulty to conclude from only statements 2 and 3 that Boots is happy. The if-then form of statement 3 is *If a cat is happy, then it purrs.*

Advertisers often use faulty logic in subtle ways to help sell their products. By studying the arguments, you can decide whether the argument is valid or faulty.

Decide if each argument is valid or faulty.

1. (1) If you buy Tuff Cote luggage, it will survive airline travel.
(2) Justin buys Tuff Cote luggage.
Conclusion: Justin's luggage will survive airline travel.

2. (1) If you buy Tuff Cote luggage, it will survive airline travel.
(2) Justin's luggage survived airline travel.
Conclusion: Justin has Tuff Cote luggage.

3. (1) If you use Clear Line long distance service, you will have clear reception.
(2) Anna has clear long distance reception.
Conclusion: Anna uses Clear Line long distance service.

4. (1) If you read the book *Beautiful Braids*, you will be able to make beautiful braids easily.
(2) Nancy read the book *Beautiful Braids*.
Conclusion: Nancy can make beautiful braids easily.

5. (1) If you buy a word processor, you will be able to write letters faster.
(2) Tania bought a word processor.
Conclusion: Tania will be able to write letters faster.

6. (1) Great swimmers wear AquaLine swimwear.
(2) Gina wears AquaLine swimwear.
Conclusion: Gina is a great swimmer.

7. Write an example of faulty logic that you have seen in an advertisement.

Valid and Faulty Arguments

Consider the statements at the right.
What conclusions can you make?

(1) Boots is a cat.
(2) Boots is purring.
(3) A cat purrs if it is happy.

From statements 1 and 3, it is correct to conclude that Boots
purrs if it is happy. However, it is faulty to conclude from only
statements 2 and 3 that Boots is happy. The if-then form of
statement 3 is *If a cat is happy, then it purrs.*

Advertisers often use faulty logic in subtle ways to help sell
their products. By studying the arguments, you can decide
whether the argument is valid or faulty.

Decide if each argument is valid or faulty.

1. (1) If you buy Tuff Cote luggage, it
   will survive airline travel.
   (2) Justin buys Tuff Cote luggage.
   Conclusion: Justin's luggage will
   survive airline travel. **valid**

2. (1) If you buy Tuff Cote luggage, it
   will survive airline travel.
   (2) Justin's luggage survived airline
   travel.
   Conclusion: Justin has Tuff Cote
   luggage. **faulty**

3. (1) If you use Clear Line long
   distance service, you will have clear
   reception.
   (2) Anna has clear long distance
   reception.
   Conclusion: Anna uses Clear Line
   long distance service. **faulty**

4. (1) If you read the book *Beautiful
   Braids*, you will be able to make
   beautiful braids easily.
   (2) Nancy read the book *Beautiful
   Braids*.
   Conclusion: Nancy can make
   beautiful braids easily. **valid**

5. (1) If you buy a word processor, you
   will be able to write letters faster.
   (2) Tania bought a word processor.
   Conclusion: Tania will be able to
   write letters faster. **valid**

6. (1) Great swimmers wear AquaLine
   swimwear.
   (2) Gina wears AquaLine swimwear.
   Conclusion: Gina is a great swimmer.
   faulty

7. Write an example of faulty logic that
   you have seen in an advertisement.
   See students' work.

1-4

Enrichment

Student Edition
Pages 19–23

Properties of Operations

Let's make up a new operation and denote it by $\circledast$, so that $a \circledast b$ means b^a.

$2 \circledast 3 = 3^2 = 9$

$(1 \circledast 2) \circledast 3 = 2^1 \circledast 3 = 3^2 = 9$

1. What number is represented by $2 \circledast 3$? _____

2. What number is represented by $3 \circledast 2$? _____

3. Does the operation $\circledast$ appear to be commutative? _____

4. What number is represented by $(2 \circledast 1) \circledast 3$? _____

5. What number is represented by $2 \circledast (1 \circledast 3)$? _____

6. Does the operation $\circledast$ appear to be associative? _____

Let's make up another operation and denote it by $\oplus$,
so that $a \oplus b = (a + 1)(b + 1)$.

$3 \oplus 2 = (3 + 1)(2 + 1) = 4 \cdot 3 = 12$

$(1 \oplus 2) \oplus 3 = (2 \cdot 3) \oplus 3 = 6 \oplus 3 = 7 \cdot 4 = 28$

7. What number is represented by $2 \oplus 3$? _____

8. What number is represented by $3 \oplus 2$? _____

9. Does the operation $\oplus$ appear to be commutative? _____

10. What number is represented by $(2 \oplus 3) \oplus 4$? _____

11. What number is represented by $2 \oplus (3 \oplus 4)$? _____

12. Does the operation $\oplus$ appear to be associative? _____

13. What number is represented by $1 \circledast (3 \oplus 2)$? _____

14. What number is represented by $(1 \circledast 3) \oplus (1 \circledast 2)$? _____

15. Does the operation $\circledast$ appear to be distributive over the operation $\oplus$? _____

16. Let's explore these operations a little further. What number is

    represented by $3 \circledast (4 \oplus 2)$? _____

17. What number is represented by $(3 \circledast 4) \oplus (3 \circledast 2)$? _____

18. Is the operation $\circledast$ actually distributive over the operation $\oplus$? _____

4   *Algebra: Concepts and Applications*

Properties of Operations

Let's make up a new operation and denote it by $\circledast$, so that $a \circledast b$ means b^a.

$2 \circledast 3 = 3^2 = 9$

$(1 \circledast 2) \circledast 3 = 2^1 \circledast 3 = 3^2 = 9$

1. What number is represented by $2 \circledast 3$? _____$3^2 = 9$_____

2. What number is represented by $3 \circledast 2$? _____$2^3 = 8$_____

3. Does the operation $\circledast$ appear to be commutative? _____no_____

4. What number is represented by $(2 \circledast 1) \circledast 3$? _____3_____

5. What number is represented by $2 \circledast (1 \circledast 3)$? _____9_____

6. Does the operation $\circledast$ appear to be associative? _____no_____

Let's make up another operation and denote it by $\oplus$, so that $a \oplus b = (a + 1)(b + 1)$.

$3 \oplus 2 = (3 + 1)(2 + 1) = 4 \cdot 3 = 12$

$(1 \oplus 2) \oplus 3 = (2 \cdot 3) \oplus 3 = 6 \oplus 3 = 7 \cdot 4 = 28$

7. What number is represented by $2 \oplus 3$? _____12_____

8. What number is represented by $3 \oplus 2$? _____12_____

9. Does the operation $\oplus$ appear to be commutative? _____yes_____

10. What number is represented by $(2 \oplus 3) \oplus 4$? _____65_____

11. What number is represented by $2 \oplus (3 \oplus 4)$? _____63_____

12. Does the operation $\oplus$ appear to be associative? _____no_____

13. What number is represented by $1 \circledast (3 \oplus 2)$? _____12_____

14. What number is represented by $(1 \circledast 3) \oplus (1 \circledast 2)$? _____12_____

15. Does the operation $\circledast$ appear to be distributive over the operation $\oplus$? _____yes_____

16. Let's explore these operations a little further. What number is

    represented by $3 \circledast (4 \oplus 2)$? _____3375_____

17. What number is represented by $(3 \circledast 4) \oplus (3 \circledast 2)$? _____585_____

18. Is the operation $\circledast$ actually distributive over the operation $\oplus$? _____no_____

1-5

Enrichment

Formulas

Some consumers use the following formula when purchasing a new car.

$$d = 0.2(4s + c)$$ where d = the price the dealer paid the factory for the new car
s = the sticker price (the factory's suggested price)
and c = the cost for dealer preparation and shipping

1. What is the dealer cost for a car with a sticker price of $12,000 and costs for preparation and shipping of $320?

2. According to this formula, how much money does a dealer make if a car is sold for its sticker price of $9500 and the dealer pays $280 for shipping and preparation?

In *The 1978 Bill James Baseball Abstract,* the author introduced the "runs created" formula.

$$R = \frac{(h + w)t}{(b + w)}$$ where h = a player's number of hits
w = a player's number of walks
t = a player's number of total bases
b = a player's number of at-bats
and R = the approximate number of runs a team scores that are due to this player's actions

3. On June 15, 1983, the Seattle Mariners traded Julio Cruz to the Chicago White Sox for Tony Bernazard. Before the trade, these were the totals for each player.

	h	w	t	b	runs created
Cruz	46	20	64	181	_____
Bernazard	61	17	87	233	_____

Find the number of runs created by each player. Which player created more runs?

4. On August 10, 1983, the New York Yankees traded Jerry Mumphrey to the Houston Astros for Omar Moreno. Before the trade, these were the totals for each player.

	h	w	t	b	runs created
Mumphrey	70	28	132	267	_____
Moreno	98	8	132	405	_____

Find the number of runs created by each player.

Formulas

Some consumers use the following formula when purchasing a new car.

$$d = 0.2(4s + c)$$ where d = the price the dealer paid the factory for the new car
s = the sticker price (the factory's suggested price)
and c = the cost for dealer preparation and shipping

1. What is the dealer cost for a car with a sticker price of
$12,000 and costs for preparation and shipping of $320? **$9664**

2. According to this formula, how much money does a dealer
make if a car is sold for its sticker price of $9500 and the
dealer pays $280 for shipping and preparation? **$1844**

In *The 1978 Bill James Baseball Abstract,* the author introduced
the "runs created" formula.

$$R = \frac{(h + w)t}{(b + w)}$$ where h = a player's number of hits
w = a player's number of walks
t = a player's number of total bases
b = a player's number of at-bats
and R = the approximate number of runs a team scores that
are due to this player's actions

3. On June 15, 1983, the Seattle Mariners traded Julio Cruz to
the Chicago White Sox for Tony Bernazard. Before the trade,
these were the totals for each player.

	h	w	t	b	runs created
Cruz	46	20	64	181	**21 runs**
Bernazard	61	17	87	233	**27 runs**

Find the number of runs created by each player. Which
player created more runs? **Bernazard**

4. On August 10, 1983, the New York Yankees traded Jerry
Mumphrey to the Houston Astros for Omar Moreno. Before
the trade, these were the totals for each player.

	h	w	t	b	runs created
Mumphrey	70	28	132	267	**44 runs**
Moreno	98	8	132	405	**34 runs**

Find the number of runs created by each player.

Latin Squares

In designing a statistical experiment, it is important to try to randomize the variables. For example, suppose 4 different motor oils are being compared to see which give the best gasoline mileage. An experimenter might then choose 4 different drivers and four different cars. To test-drive all the possible combinations, the experimenter would need 64 test-drives.

To reduce the number of test drives, a statistician might use an arrangement called a **Latin Square**.

For this example, the four motor oils are labeled A, B, C, and D and are arranged as shown. Each oil must appear exactly one time in each row and column of the square.

The drivers are labeled D(1), D(2), D(3), and D(4); the cars are labeled C(1), C(2), C(3), and C(4).

	D(1)	D(2)	D(3)	D(4)
C(1)	A	B	C	D
C(2)	B	A	D	C
C(3)	C	D	A	B
C(4)	D	C	B	A

Now, the number of test-drives is just 16, one for each cell of the Latin Square.

Create two 4-by-4 Latin Squares that are different from the example.

1.

	D(1)	D(2)	D(3)	D(4)
C(1)				
C(2)				
C(3)				
C(4)				

2.

	D(1)	D(2)	D(3)	D(4)
C(1)				
C(2)				
C(3)				
C(4)				

Make three different 3-by-3 Latin Squares.

3.

	D(1)	D(2)	D(3)
C(1)			
C(2)			
C(3)			

4.

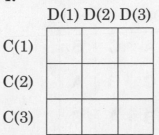

	D(1)	D(2)	D(3)
C(1)			
C(2)			
C(3)			

5.

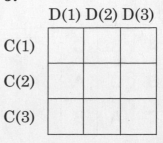

	D(1)	D(2)	D(3)
C(1)			
C(2)			
C(3)			

1-6

Enrichment

Latin Squares

In designing a statistical experiment, it is important to try to randomize the variables. For example, suppose 4 different motor oils are being compared to see which give the best gasoline mileage. An experimenter might then choose 4 different drivers and four different cars. To test-drive all the possible combinations, the experimenter would need 64 test-drives.

To reduce the number of test drives, a statistician might use an arrangement called a **Latin Square**.

For this example, the four motor oils are labeled A, B, C, and D and are arranged as shown. Each oil must appear exactly one time in each row and column of the square.

The drivers are labeled D(1), D(2), D(3), and D(4); the cars are labeled C(1), C(2), C(3), and C(4).

	D(1)	D(2)	D(3)	D(4)
C(1)	A	B	C	D
C(2)	B	A	D	C
C(3)	C	D	A	B
C(4)	D	C	B	A

Now, the number of test-drives is just 16, one for each cell of the Latin Square.

Create two 4-by-4 Latin Squares that are different from the example. Sample answers are given.

1.

	D(1)	D(2)	D(3)	D(4)
C(1)	B	C	A	D
C(2)	D	A	C	B
C(3)	C	D	B	A
C(4)	A	B	D	C

2.

	D(1)	D(2)	D(3)	D(4)
C(1)	D	C	B	A
C(2)	A	B	C	D
C(3)	B	D	A	C
C(4)	C	A	D	B

Make three different 3-by-3 Latin Squares.

3.

	D(1)	D(2)	D(3)
C(1)	A	B	C
C(2)	B	C	A
C(3)	C	A	B

4.

	D(1)	D(2)	D(3)
C(1)	A	C	B
C(2)	C	B	A
C(3)	B	A	C

5.

	D(1)	D(2)	D(3)
C(1)	B	C	A
C(2)	C	A	B
C(3)	A	B	C

1-7

Enrichment

The Digits of π

The number π (pi) is the ratio of the circumference of a circle to its diameter. It is a nonrepeating and nonterminating decimal. No block of the digits of π ever repeats. Here are the first 201 digits of π including 200 digits that follow the decimal point.

3.14159	26535	89793	23846
69399	37510	58209	74944
86280	34825	34211	70679
09384	46095	50582	23172
84102	70193	85211	05559
26433	83279	50288	41971
59230	78164	06286	20899
82148	08651	32823	06647
53594	08128	34111	74502
64462	29489	54930	38196

Solve each problem.

1. If each of the digits appeared with equal frequency, how many times would each digit appear in the first 200 places following the decimal point?

2. Complete this frequency distribution table for the first 200 digits of π that follow the decimal point.

Digit	Frequency (Tally Marks)	Frequency (Number)	Cumulative Frequency
0			
1			
2			
3			
4			
5			
6			
7			
8			
9			

3. Explain how the cumulative frequency column can be used to check a project like this one.

4. Which digit(s) appears most often?

5. Which digit(s) appears least often?

Algebra: Concepts and Applications

Enrichment

The Digits of π

The number π (pi) is the ratio of the circumference of a circle to its diameter. It is a nonrepeating and nonterminating decimal. No block of the digits of π ever repeats. Here are the first 201 digits of π including 200 digits that follow the decimal point.

3.14159	26535	89793	23846
69399	37510	58209	74944
86280	34825	34211	70679
09384	46095	50582	23172
84102	70193	85211	05559
26433	83279	50288	41971
59230	78164	06286	20899
82148	08651	32823	06647
53594	08128	34111	74502
64462	29489	54930	38196

Solve each problem.

1. If each of the digits appeared with equal frequency, how many times would each digit appear in the first 200 places following the decimal point? **20**

2. Complete this frequency distribution table for the first 200 digits of π that follow the decimal point.

Digit	Frequency (Tally Marks)	Frequency (Number)	Cumulative Frequency
0	⁄⁄⁄⁄ ⁄⁄⁄⁄ ⁄⁄⁄⁄ ////	19	19
1	⁄⁄⁄⁄ ⁄⁄⁄⁄ ⁄⁄⁄⁄ ⁄⁄⁄⁄	20	39
2	⁄⁄⁄⁄ ⁄⁄⁄⁄ ⁄⁄⁄⁄ ⁄⁄⁄⁄ ////	24	63
3	⁄⁄⁄⁄ ⁄⁄⁄⁄ ⁄⁄⁄⁄ ⁄⁄⁄⁄	20	83
4	⁄⁄⁄⁄ ⁄⁄⁄⁄ ⁄⁄⁄⁄ ⁄⁄⁄⁄ //	22	105
5	⁄⁄⁄⁄ ⁄⁄⁄⁄ ⁄⁄⁄⁄ ⁄⁄⁄⁄	20	125
6	⁄⁄⁄⁄ ⁄⁄⁄⁄ ⁄⁄⁄⁄ /	16	141
7	⁄⁄⁄⁄ ⁄⁄⁄⁄ //	12	153
8	⁄⁄⁄⁄ ⁄⁄⁄⁄ ⁄⁄⁄⁄ ⁄⁄⁄⁄ ////	24	177
9	⁄⁄⁄⁄ ⁄⁄⁄⁄ ⁄⁄⁄⁄ ⁄⁄⁄⁄ ///	23	200

3. Explain how the cumulative frequency column can be used to check a project like this one. **The last number should be 200, the number of items being counted.**

4. Which digit(s) appears most often? **2 and 8**

5. Which digit(s) appears least often? **7**

Venn Diagrams

A type of drawing called a **Venn diagram** can be useful in explaining conditional statements. A Venn diagram uses circles to represent sets of objects.

Consider the statement "All rabbits have long ears." To make a Venn diagram for this statement, a large circle is drawn to represent all animals with long ears. Then a smaller circle is drawn inside the first to represent all rabbits. The Venn diagram shows that every rabbit is included in the group of long-eared animals.

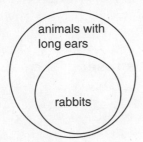

The set of rabbits is called a **subset** of the set of long-eared animals.

The Venn diagram can also explain how to write the statement, "All rabbits have long ears," in if-then form. Every rabbit is in the group of long-eared animals, so if an animal is a rabbit, then it has long ears.

For each statement, draw a Venn diagram. The write the sentence in if-then form.

1. Every dog has long hair.

2. All rational numbers are real.

3. People who live in Iowa like corn.

4. Staff members are allowed in the faculty lounge.

Enrichment

Venn Diagrams

A type of drawing called a **Venn diagram** can be useful in explaining conditional statements. A Venn diagram uses circles to represent sets of objects.

Consider the statement "All rabbits have long ears." To make a Venn diagram for this statement, a large circle is drawn to represent all animals with long ears. Then a smaller circle is drawn inside the first to represent all rabbits. The Venn diagram shows that every rabbit is included in the group of long-eared animals.

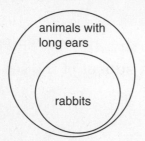

The set of rabbits is called a **subset** of the set of long-eared animals.

The Venn diagram can also explain how to write the statement, "All rabbits have long ears," in if-then form. Every rabbit is in the group of long-eared animals, so if an animal is a rabbit, then it has long ears.

For each statement, draw a Venn diagram. The write the sentence in if-then form.

1. Every dog has long hair.

If an animal is a dog, then it has long hair.

2. All rational numbers are real.

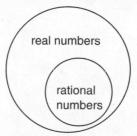

If a number is rational, then it is real.

3. People who live in Iowa like corn.

If a person lives in Iowa, then the person likes corn.

4. Staff members are allowed in the faculty lounge.

If a person is a staff member, then the person is allowed in the faculty cafeteria.

Algebra: Concepts and Applications

2-2

Enrichment

Points and Lines on a Matrix

A **matrix** is a rectangular array of rows and columns. Points and lines on a matrix are not defined in the same way as in Euclidean geometry. A **point** on a matrix is a dot, which can be small or large. A **line** on a matrix is a path of dots that "line up." Between two points on a line there may or may not be other points. Three examples of lines are shown at the upper right. The broad line can be thought of as a single line or as two narrow lines side by side.

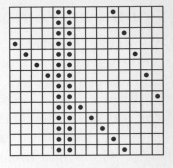

A dot-matrix printer for a computer uses dots to form characters. The dots are often called **pixels**. The matrix at the right shows how a dot-matrix printer might print the letter P.

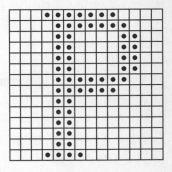

Draw points on each matrix to create the given figures.

1. Draw two intersecting lines that have four points in common.

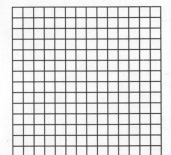

2. Draw two lines that cross but have no common points.

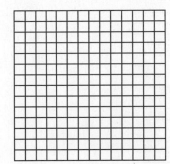

3. Make the number 0 (zero) so that it extends to the top and bottom sides of the matrix.

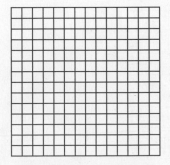

4. Make the capital letter O so that it extends to each side of the matrix.

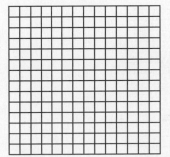

5. Using separate grid paper, make dot designs for several other letters. Which were the easiest and which were the most difficult?

9

Algebra: Concepts and Applications

NAME _____ DATE _____ PERIOD _____

Enrichment

Points and Lines on a Matrix

A **matrix** is a rectangular array of rows and columns. Points and lines on a matrix are not defined in the same way as in Euclidean geometry. A **point** on a matrix is a dot, which can be small or large. A **line** on a matrix is a path of dots that "line up." Between two points on a line there may or may not be other points. Three examples of lines are shown at the upper right. The broad line can be thought of as a single line or as two narrow lines side by side.

A dot-matrix printer for a computer uses dots to form characters. The dots are often called **pixels**. The matrix at the right shows how a dot-matrix printer might print the letter P.

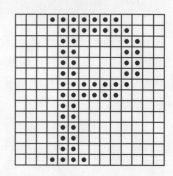

Sample answers are given.
Draw points on each matrix to create the given figures.

1. Draw two intersecting lines that have four points in common.

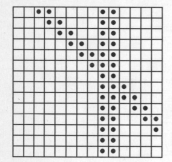

2. Draw two lines that cross but have no common points.

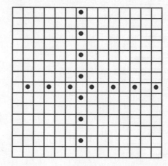

3. Make the number 0 (zero) so that it extends to the top and bottom sides of the matrix.

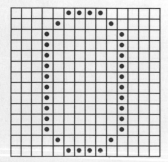

4. Make the capital letter O so that it extends to each side of the matrix.

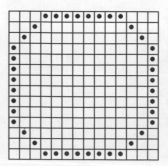

5. Using separate grid paper, make dot designs for several other letters. Which were the easiest and which were the most difficult? **See students' work.**

     Algebra: Concepts and Applications

Enrichment

Student Edition
Pages 64–69

Integer Magic

A **magic triangle** is a triangular arrangement of numbers in which the sum of the numbers along each side is the same number. For example, in the magic triangle shown at the right, the sum of the numbers along each side is 0.

In each triangle, each of the integers from −4 to 4 appears exactly once. Complete the triangle so that the sum of the integers along each side is −3.

1.

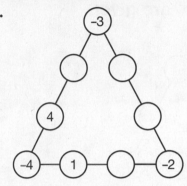

2.

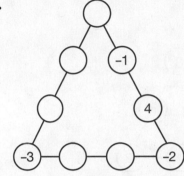

3.

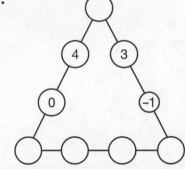

4.

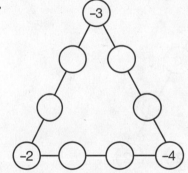

In these magic stars, the sum of the integers along each line of the star is −2. Complete each magic star using the integers from −6 to 5 exactly once.

5.

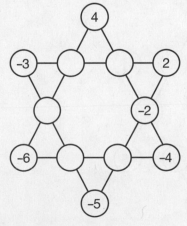

6.

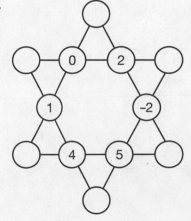

Algebra: Concepts and Applications

Integer Magic

A **magic triangle** is a triangular arrangement of numbers in which the sum of the numbers along each side is the same number. For example, in the magic triangle shown at the right, the sum of the numbers along each side is 0.

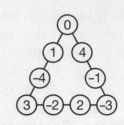

In each triangle, each of the integers from −4 to 4 appears exactly once. Complete the triangle so that the sum of the integers along each side is −3.

Sample answers are given.

1.

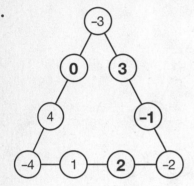

2.

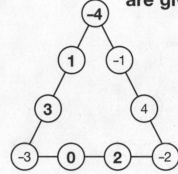

3.

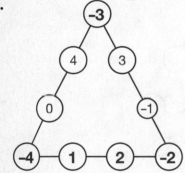

4.

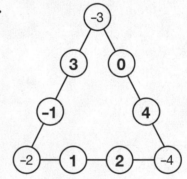

In these magic stars, the sum of the integers along each line of the star is −2. Complete each magic star using the integers from −6 to 5 exactly once.

5.

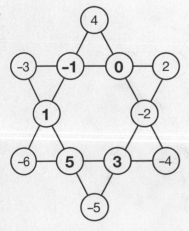

6.

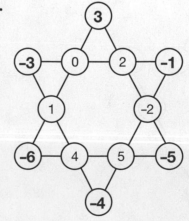

T10 *Algebra: Concepts and Applications*

Closure

A **binary operation** matches two numbers in a set to just one number. Addition is a binary operation on the set of whole numbers. It matches two numbers such as 4 and 5 to a single number, their sum.

If the result of a binary operation is always a member of the original set, the set is said to be **closed** under the operation. For example, the set of whole numbers is not closed under subtraction because $3 - 6$ is not a whole number.

Is each operation binary? Write yes or no.

1. the operation $\hookleftarrow$, where $a \hookleftarrow b$ means to choose the lesser number from a and b

2. the operation ©, where $a © b$ means to cube the sum of a and b

3. the operation sq, where $sq(a)$ means to square the number a

4. the operation exp, where $exp(a, b)$ means to find the value of a^b

5. the operation $\Uparrow$, where $a \Uparrow b$ means to match a and b to any number greater than either number

6. the operation $\Rightarrow$, where $a \Rightarrow b$ means to round the product of a and b up to the nearest 10

Is each set closed under addition? Write yes or no. If your answer is no, give an example.

7. even numbers

8. odd numbers

9. multiples of 3

10. multiples of 5

11. prime numbers

12. nonprime numbers

Is the set of whole numbers closed under each operation? Write yes or no. If your answer is no, give an example.

13. multiplication: $a \times b$

14. division: $a \div b$

15. exponentation: a^b

16. squaring the sum: $(a + b)^2$

Enrichment

Closure

A **binary operation** matches two numbers in a set to just one number. Addition is a binary operation on the set of whole numbers. It matches two numbers such as 4 and 5 to a single number, their sum.

If the result of a binary operation is always a member of the original set, the set is said to be **closed** under the operation. For example, the set of whole numbers is not closed under subtraction because $3 - 6$ is not a whole number.

Is each operation binary? Write yes or no.

1. the operation $\hookleftarrow$, where $a \hookleftarrow b$ means to choose the lesser number from a and b **yes**

2. the operation ©, where $a © b$ means to cube the sum of a and b **yes**

3. the operation sq, where $sq(a)$ means to square the number a **no**

4. the operation exp, where $exp(a, b)$ means to find the value of a^b **yes**

5. the operation $\Uparrow$, where $a \Uparrow b$ means to match a and b to any number greater than either number **no**

6. the operation $\Rightarrow$, where $a \Rightarrow b$ means to round the product of a and b up to the nearest 10 **yes**

Is each set closed under addition? Write yes or no. If your answer is no, give an example.

7. even numbers **yes**

8. odd numbers **no; 3 + 7 = 10**

9. multiples of 3 **yes**

10. multiples of 5 **yes**

11. prime numbers **no; 3 + 5 = 8**

12. nonprime numbers **no; 22 + 9 = 31**

Is the set of whole numbers closed under each operation? Write yes or no. If your answer is no, give an example.

13. multiplication: $a \times b$ **yes**

14. division: $a \div b$ **no; 4 ÷ 3 is not a whole number**

15. exponentiation: a^b **yes**

16. squaring the sum: $(a + b)^2$ **yes**

2-5 Enrichment

Student Edition
Pages 75–79

The Binary Number System

Our standard number system in base ten has ten digits, 0 through 9. In base ten, the values of the places are powers of 10.

A system of numeration that is used in computer technology is the **binary number system**. In a **binary number**, the place value of each digit is two times the place value of the digit to its right. There are only two digits in the binary system: 0 and 1.

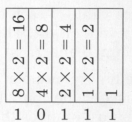

The binary number 10111 is written 10111_{two}. You can use a place-value chart like the one at the right to find the standard number that is equivalent to this number.

$$10111_{two} = 1 \times 16 + 0 \times 8 + 1 \times 4 + 1 \times 2 + 1 \times 1$$
$$= 16 + 0 + 4 + 2 + 1$$
$$= 23$$

Write each binary number as a standard number.

1. 11_{two} **2.** 111_{two} **3.** 100_{two}

4. 1001_{two} **5.** 11001_{two} **6.** 100101_{two}

Write each standard number as a binary number.

7. 8   **8.** 10   **9.** 15

10. 17   **11.** 28   **12.** 34

Write each answer as a binary number.

13. $1_{two} + 10_{two}$ **14.** $101_{two} - 10_{two}$

15. $10_{two} \times 11_{two}$ **16.** $10000_{two} \div 10_{two}$

17. What standard number is equivalent to 12021_{three}?

          Algebra: Concepts and Applications

2-5

Enrichment

The Binary Number System

Our standard number system in base ten has ten digits,
0 through 9. In base ten, the values of the places are
powers of 10.

A system of numeration that is used in computer technology
is the **binary number system**. In a **binary number**, the
place value of each digit is two times the place value of the
digit to its right. There are only two digits in the binary
system: 0 and 1.

The binary number 10111 is written 10111_{two}. You can use
a place-value chart like the one at the right to find the
standard number that is equivalent to this number.

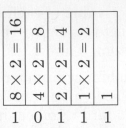

$$10111_{two} = 1 \times 16 + 0 \times 8 + 1 \times 4 + 1 \times 2 + 1 \times 1$$
$$= 16 + 0 + 4 + 2 + 1$$
$$= 23$$

Write each binary number as a standard number.

1. 11_{two} **3**

2. 111_{two} **7**

3. 100_{two} **4**

4. 1001_{two} **9**

5. 11001_{two} **25**

6. 100101_{two} **37**

Write each standard number as a binary number.

7. 8 **1000_{two}**

8. 10 **1010_{two}**

9. 15 **1111_{two}**

10. 17 **10001_{two}**

11. 28 **11100_{two}**

12. 34 **100010_{two}**

Write each answer as a binary number.

13. $1_{two} + 10_{two}$ **11_{two}**

14. $101_{two} - 10_{two}$ **11_{two}**

15. $10_{two} \times 11_{two}$ **110_{two}**

16. $10000_{two} \div 10_{two}$ **1000_{two}**

17. What standard number is equivalent to 12021_{three}? **142**

2-6 **Enrichment**

Day of the Week Formula

The following formula can be used to determine the specific day of the week on which a date occurred.

$$s = d + 2m + [(3m + 3) \div 5] + y + \left[\frac{y}{4}\right] - \left[\frac{y}{100}\right] + \left[\frac{y}{100}\right] + 2$$

s = sum
d = day of the month, using numbers from 1–31
m = month, beginning with March is 3, April is 4, and so on, up to December is 12, January is 13, and February is 14
y = year except for dates in January or February when the previous year is used

For example, for February 13, 1985, $d = 13$, $m = 14$, and $y = 1984$; and for July 4, 1776, $d = 4$, $m = 7$, and $y = 1776$

The brackets, [ ], mean you are to do the division inside them, discard the remainder, and use only the whole number part of the quotient. The next step is to divide s by 7 and note the remainder. The remainder 0 is Saturday, 1 is Sunday, 2 is Monday, and so on, up to 6 is Friday.

Example: What day of the week was October 3, 1854?

For October 3, 1854, $d = 3$, $m = 10$, and $y = 1854$.

$$s = 3 + \underbrace{[\,2(10)\,]}_{} + \underbrace{[\,(3 \times 10 + 3) \div 5\,]}_{} + 1854 + \left[\frac{1854}{4}\right] - \left[\frac{1854}{100}\right] + \left[\frac{1854}{400}\right] + 2$$

$$= 3 + \quad 20 \quad + \quad\quad 6 \quad\quad + 1854 + \quad 463 \quad - \quad 18 \quad + \quad 4 \quad + 2$$

$$= 2334$$

$s \div 7 = 2334 \div 7$
$\quad\quad\quad = 333 \text{ R}3$

Since the remainder is 3, the day of the week was Tuesday.

Solve.

1. See if the formula works for today's date.

2. On what day of the week were you born?

3. What will be the day of the week on April 13, 2006?

4. On what day of the week was July 4, 1776?

2-6

Enrichment

Day of the Week Formula

The following formula can be used to determine the specific day of the week on which a date occurred.

$$s = d + 2m + [(3m + 3) \div 5] + y + \left[\frac{y}{4}\right] - \left[\frac{y}{100}\right] + \left[\frac{y}{100}\right] + 2$$

s = sum
d = day of the month, using numbers from 1–31
m = month, beginning with March is 3, April is 4, and so on, up to December is 12, January is 13, and February is 14
y = year except for dates in January or February when the previous year is used

For example, for February 13, 1985, $d = 13$, $m = 14$, and $y = 1984$; and for July 4, 1776, $d = 4$, $m = 7$, and $y = 1776$

The brackets, [ ], mean you are to do the division inside them, discard the remainder, and use only the whole number part of the quotient. The next step is to divide s by 7 and note the remainder. The remainder 0 is Saturday, 1 is Sunday, 2 is Monday, and so on, up to 6 is Friday.

Example: What day of the week was October 3, 1854?

For October 3, 1854, $d = 3$, $m = 10$, and $y = 1854$.

$$s = 3 + [\underbrace{2(10)}] + [\underbrace{(3 \times 10 + 3) \div 5}] + 1854 + \left[\frac{1854}{4}\right] - \left[\frac{1854}{100}\right] + \left[\frac{1854}{400}\right] + 2$$

$$= 3 + \quad 20 \quad + \quad\quad 6 \quad\quad + 1854 + 463 - 18 + 4 + 2$$

$$= 2334$$

$$s \div 7 = 2334 \div 7$$
$$= 333 \text{ R3}$$

Since the remainder is 3, the day of the week was Tuesday.

Solve.

1. See if the formula works for today's date. **Answers will vary.**

2. On what day of the week were you born? **Answers will vary.**

3. What will be the day of the week on April 13, 2006?

$$s = 13 + 2(4) + [(3 \times 4 + 3) \div 5] + 2006 + \left[\frac{2006}{4}\right] - \left[\frac{2006}{100}\right] + \left[\frac{2006}{400}\right] + 2$$

$= 13 + 8 + 3 + 2006 + 501 - 20 + 4 + 2 = 2518$; $2518 \div 7 = 359$ R5   **Thursday**

4. On what day of the week was July 4, 1776?

$$s = 4 + 2(7) + [(3 \times 7 + 3) \div 5] + 1776 + \left[\frac{1776}{4}\right] - \left[\frac{1776}{100}\right] + \left[\frac{1776}{400}\right] + 2$$

$= 4 + 14 + 4 + 1776 + 444 - 17 + 4 + 2 = 2231$; $2231 \div 7 = 318$ R5   **Thursday**

3-1 Enrichment

Matching Equivalent Fractions

Cut out the pieces below and match the edges so that equivalent fractions meet. The pieces form a rectangle. The outer edges of the rectangle formed will have no fractions on them.

Row 1:
- Piece 1: top $\frac{9}{10}$, left $\frac{15}{35}$, right $\frac{5}{9}$, bottom $\frac{3}{24}$
- Piece 2: top $\frac{1}{7}$, left $\frac{12}{42}$, right $\frac{3}{8}$, bottom $\frac{2}{10}$
- Piece 3: top $\frac{11}{12}$, left $\frac{16}{28}$, right $\frac{5}{8}$, bottom $\frac{45}{50}$
- Piece 4: top $\frac{12}{13}$, left $\frac{8}{20}$, right $\frac{4}{7}$, bottom $\frac{40}{45}$
- Piece 5: top $\frac{8}{9}$, left $\frac{5}{15}$, right $\frac{3}{7}$, bottom $\frac{3}{21}$

Row 2:
- Piece 1: top $\frac{9}{11}$, left $\frac{15}{21}$, bottom $\frac{40}{44}$
- Piece 2: top $\frac{3}{10}$, right $\frac{1}{2}$, bottom $\frac{52}{56}$
- Piece 3: top $\frac{1}{9}$, left $\frac{35}{77}$, right $\frac{7}{13}$
- Piece 4: top $\frac{1}{8}$, left $\frac{18}{48}$, right $\frac{4}{9}$, bottom $\frac{2}{18}$
- Piece 5: left $\frac{8}{10}$, right $\frac{27}{33}$

Row 3:
- Piece 1: top $\frac{1}{12}$, left $\frac{24}{54}$, bottom $\frac{2}{20}$
- Piece 2: top $\frac{1}{10}$, left $\frac{49}{91}$
- Piece 3: left $\frac{6}{8}$, right $\frac{4}{5}$, bottom $\frac{21}{33}$
- Piece 4: top $\frac{7}{8}$, right $\frac{1}{3}$, bottom $\frac{3}{18}$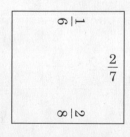
- Piece 5: top $\frac{7}{11}$, left $\frac{9}{15}$, right $\frac{5}{7}$, bottom $\frac{44}{48}$

Row 4:
- Piece 1: left $\frac{4}{6}$, right $\frac{3}{4}$, bottom $\frac{9}{33}$
- Piece 2: top $\frac{1}{5}$, left $\frac{14}{56}$, right $\frac{5}{11}$
- Piece 3: top $\frac{1}{4}$, right $\frac{2}{8}$
- Piece 4: top $\frac{1}{6}$, right $\frac{2}{7}$, bottom $\frac{2}{8}$
- Piece 5: top $\frac{13}{14}$, right $\frac{2}{5}$, bottom $\frac{35}{40}$

Row 5:
- Piece 1: right $\frac{2}{3}$, bottom $\frac{6}{20}$
- Piece 2: top $\frac{6}{7}$, left $\frac{25}{45}$, bottom $\frac{3}{36}$
- Piece 3: (blank)
- Piece 4: top $\frac{3}{11}$, left $\frac{3}{6}$, right $\frac{3}{5}$, bottom $\frac{48}{52}$
- Piece 5: top $\frac{10}{11}$, left $\frac{20}{32}$, bottom $\frac{30}{35}$

Algebra: Concepts and Applications

NAME _____ DATE _____ PERIOD _____

Enrichment

Student Edition
Pages 94–99

Matching Equivalent Fractions

Cut out the pieces below and match the edges so that equivalent fractions meet. The pieces form a rectangle. The outer edges of the rectangle formed will have no fractions on them.

Piece 15: top $\frac{9}{10}$, left $\frac{15}{35}$, right $\frac{5}{9}$, bottom $\frac{3}{24}$

Piece 18: top $\frac{1}{7}$, left $\frac{12}{42}$, right $\frac{3}{8}$, bottom $\frac{2}{10}$

Piece 11: top $\frac{11}{12}$, left $\frac{16}{28}$, right $\frac{5}{8}$, bottom $\frac{45}{50}$

Piece 10: top $\frac{12}{13}$, left $\frac{8}{20}$, right $\frac{4}{7}$, bottom $\frac{40}{45}$

Piece 14: top $\frac{8}{9}$, left $\frac{5}{15}$, right $\frac{3}{7}$, bottom $\frac{3}{21}$

Piece 8: top $\frac{9}{11}$, left $\frac{15}{21}$, bottom $\frac{40}{44}$

Piece 5: top $\frac{3}{10}$, right $\frac{1}{2}$, bottom $\frac{52}{56}$

Piece 23: top $\frac{1}{9}$, left $\frac{35}{77}$, right $\frac{7}{13}$

Piece 19: top $\frac{1}{8}$, left $\frac{18}{48}$, right $\frac{4}{9}$, bottom $\frac{2}{18}$

Piece 4: left $\frac{8}{10}$, bottom $\frac{27}{33}$

Piece 20: top $\frac{1}{12}$, left $\frac{24}{54}$, bottom $\frac{2}{20}$

Piece 24: top $\frac{1}{10}$, left $\frac{49}{91}$

Piece 3: left $\frac{6}{8}$, right $\frac{4}{5}$, bottom $\frac{21}{33}$

Piece 13: top $\frac{7}{8}$, right $\frac{1}{3}$, bottom $\frac{3}{18}$

Piece 7: top $\frac{7}{11}$, left $\frac{9}{15}$, right $\frac{5}{7}$, bottom $\frac{44}{48}$

Piece 2: left $\frac{4}{6}$, right $\frac{3}{4}$, bottom $\frac{9}{33}$

Piece 22: top $\frac{1}{5}$, left $\frac{14}{56}$, right $\frac{5}{11}$

Piece 21: top $\frac{1}{4}$, right $\frac{2}{8}$

Piece 17: top $\frac{1}{6}$, right $\frac{2}{7}$, bottom $\frac{2}{8}$

Piece 9: top $\frac{13}{14}$, right $\frac{2}{5}$, bottom $\frac{35}{40}$

Piece 1: right $\frac{2}{3}$, bottom $\frac{6}{20}$

Piece 16: top $\frac{6}{7}$, left $\frac{25}{45}$, bottom $\frac{3}{36}$

Piece 6: top $\frac{3}{11}$, left $\frac{3}{6}$, right $\frac{3}{5}$, bottom $\frac{48}{52}$

Piece 12: top $\frac{10}{11}$, left $\frac{20}{32}$, bottom $\frac{30}{35}$

1	2	3	4
5	6	7	8
9	10	11	12
13	14	15	16
17	18	19	20
21	22	23	24

Algebra: Concepts and Applications

3-2

Enrichment

Rounding Fractions

Rounding fractions is more difficult than rounding whole numbers or decimals. For example, think about how you would round

inches to the nearest quarter-inch. Through estimation, you might realize that $\frac{4}{9}$ is less than $\frac{1}{2}$. But, is it closer to $\frac{1}{2}$ or to $\frac{1}{4}$? Here are two ways to round fractions. Example 1 uses only the fractions; Example 2 uses decimals.

Example 1:

Subtract the fraction twice. Use the two nearest quarters.

$$\frac{1}{2} - \frac{4}{9} = \frac{1}{18} \qquad \frac{4}{9} - \frac{1}{4} = \frac{7}{36}$$

Compare the differences.

$$\frac{1}{18} < \frac{7}{36}$$

The smaller difference shows you which fraction to round to.

$\frac{4}{9}$ rounds to $\frac{1}{2}$.

Example 2:

Change the fraction and the two nearest quarters to decimals.

$$\frac{4}{9} = 0.4\overline{4}, \frac{1}{2} = 0.5, \frac{1}{4} = 0.25$$

Find the decimal halfway between the two nearest quarters.

$$\frac{1}{2}(0.5 + 0.25) = 0.375$$

If the fraction is greater than the halfway decimal, round up. If not, round down.

$0.4\overline{4} > 0.3675$. So, $\frac{4}{9}$ is more than half way between $\frac{1}{4}$ and $\frac{1}{2}$.

$\frac{4}{9}$ rounds to $\frac{1}{2}$.

Round each fraction to the nearest one-quarter. Use either method.

1. $\frac{1}{3}$

2. $\frac{3}{7}$

3. $\frac{7}{11}$

4. $\frac{4}{15}$

5. $\frac{7}{20}$

6. $\frac{31}{50}$

7. $\frac{9}{25}$

8. $\frac{23}{30}$

Round each decimal or fraction to the nearest one-eighth.

9. 0.6

10. 0.1

11. 0.45

12. 0.85

13. $\frac{5}{7}$

14. $\frac{3}{20}$

15. $\frac{23}{25}$

16. $\frac{5}{9}$

3-2 Enrichment

Student Edition
Pages 100–103

Rounding Fractions

Rounding fractions is more difficult than rounding whole numbers or decimals. For example, think about how you would round inches to the nearest quarter-inch. Through estimation, you might realize that $\frac{4}{9}$ is less than $\frac{1}{2}$. But, is it closer to $\frac{1}{2}$ or to $\frac{1}{4}$? Here are two ways to round fractions. Example 1 uses only the fractions; Example 2 uses decimals.

Example 1:

Subtract the fraction twice. Use the two nearest quarters.

$$\frac{1}{2} - \frac{4}{9} = \frac{1}{18} \qquad \frac{4}{9} - \frac{1}{4} = \frac{7}{36}$$

Compare the differences.

$$\frac{1}{18} < \frac{7}{36}$$

The smaller difference shows you which fraction to round to.

$\frac{4}{9}$ rounds to $\frac{1}{2}$.

Example 2:

Change the fraction and the two nearest quarters to decimals.

$$\frac{4}{9} = 0.4\overline{4}, \frac{1}{2} = 0.5, \frac{1}{4} = 0.25$$

Find the decimal halfway between the two nearest quarters.

$$\frac{1}{2}(0.5 + 0.25) = 0.375$$

If the fraction is greater than the halfway decimal, round up. If not, round down.

$0.4\overline{4} > 0.3675$. So, $\frac{4}{9}$ is more than half way between $\frac{1}{4}$ and $\frac{1}{2}$.

$\frac{4}{9}$ rounds to $\frac{1}{2}$.

Round each fraction to the nearest one-quarter. Use either method.

1. $\frac{1}{3}$ **$\frac{1}{4}$**

2. $\frac{3}{7}$ **$\frac{1}{2}$**

3. $\frac{7}{11}$ **$\frac{3}{4}$**

4. $\frac{4}{15}$ **$\frac{1}{4}$**

5. $\frac{7}{20}$ **$\frac{1}{4}$**

6. $\frac{31}{50}$ **$\frac{1}{2}$**

7. $\frac{9}{25}$ **$\frac{1}{4}$**

8. $\frac{23}{30}$ **$\frac{3}{4}$**

Round each decimal or fraction to the nearest one-eighth.

9. 0.6 **$\frac{5}{8}$**

10. 0.1 **$\frac{1}{8}$**

11. 0.45 **$\frac{1}{2}$**

12. 0.85 **$\frac{7}{8}$**

13. $\frac{5}{7}$ **$\frac{3}{4}$**

14. $\frac{3}{20}$ **$\frac{1}{8}$**

15. $\frac{23}{25}$ **$\frac{7}{8}$**

16. $\frac{5}{9}$ **$\frac{1}{2}$**

Algebra: Concepts and Applications

3-3

Enrichment

Student Edition
Pages 104–109

Frequency Polygons

Histigrams are often used to display frequency distributions. A **frequency polygon** can also be used. In the graphs below, a histogram is shown on the left; a frequency polygon on the right. The vertical lines drawn on the frequency polygon show the locations of the median and mode.

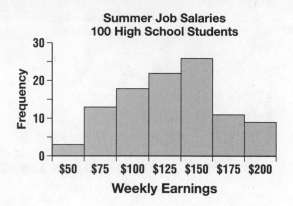

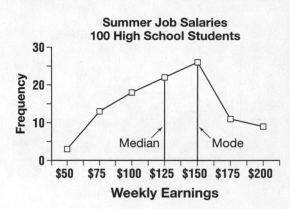

Show the median and the mode(s) on each frequency polygon.

1.

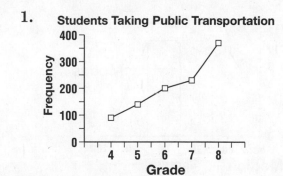

2.

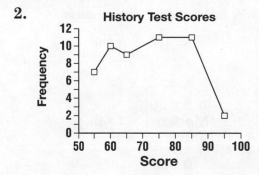

3.

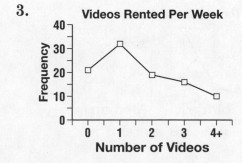

4.

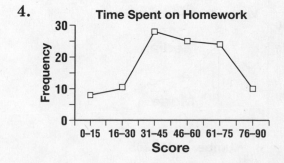

Algebra: Concepts and Applications

Enrichment

Frequency Polygons

Histigrams are often used to display frequency distributions.
A **frequency polygon** can also be used. In the graphs below,
a histogram is shown on the left; a frequency polygon on the
right. The vertical lines drawn on the frequency polygon show
the locations of the median and mode.

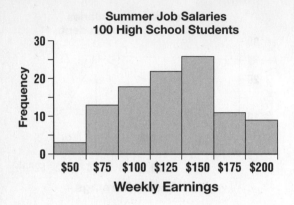

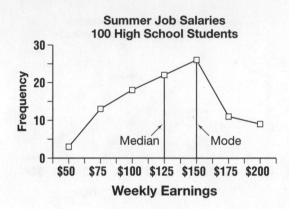

Show the median and the mode(s) on each frequency polygon.

1.

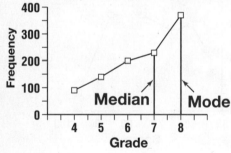

2.

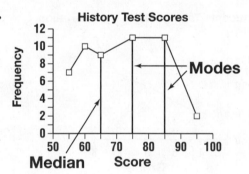

3.

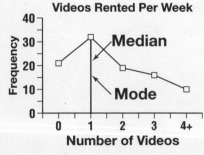

4.

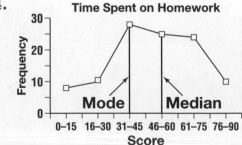

T16

Algebra: Concepts and Applications

3-4 **Enrichment**

Solution Sets

Consider the following open sentence.

It is the tallest building in the world.

You know that a replacement for the variable *It* must be found in order to determine if the sentence is true or false. If *It* is replaced by either the Empire State Building or the Sears Tower, the sentence is true.

The set {Empire State Building, Sears Tower} is called the **solution set** of the open sentence given above. This set includes all replacements for the variable that make the sentence true.

Write the solution set of each open sentence.

1. It is the name of a state beginning with the letter A.

1. _____

2. It is a primary color.

2. _____

3. Its capital is Harrisburg.

3. _____

4. It is a New England state.

4. _____

5. $x + 4 = 10$

5. _____

6. It is the name of a month that contains the letter *r*.

6. _____

7. During the 1970s, she was the wife of a U.S. President.

7. _____

8. It is an even number between 1 and 13.

8. _____

9. $31 = 72 - k$

9. _____

10. It is the square of 2, 3, or 4.

10. _____

Write an open sentence for each solution set.

11. {A, E, I, O, U}

11. _____

12. {1, 3, 5, 7, 9}

12. _____

13. {June, July, August}

13. _____

14. {Atlantic, Pacific, Indian, Arctic}

14. _____

17

Solution Sets

Consider the following open sentence.

It is the tallest building in the world.

You know that a replacement for the variable *It* must be found in order to determine if the sentence is true or false. If *It* is replaced by either the Empire State Building or the Sears Tower, the sentence is true.

The set {Empire State Building, Sears Tower} is called the **solution set** of the open sentence given above. This set includes all replacements for the variable that make the sentence true.

Write the solution set of each open sentence.

1. It is the name of a state beginning with the letter A.

1. ___{Alabama, Alaska, Arizona, Arkansas}___

2. It is a primary color.

2. ___{red, yellow, blue}___

3. Its capital is Harrisburg.

3. ___{Pennsylvania}___

4. It is a New England state.

4. ___{Maine, New Hamp., Vermont, Mass., Rhode Is., Conn.}___

5. $x + 4 = 10$

5. ___{6}___

6. It is the name of a month that contains the letter *r*.

6. ___{Jan, Feb, Mar, Apr, Sept, Oct, Nov, Dec}___

7. During the 1970s, she was the wife of a U.S. President.

7. ___{Pat Nixon, Betty Ford, Rosalyn Carter}___

8. It is an even number between 1 and 13.

8. ___{2, 4, 6, 8, 10,12}___

9. $31 = 72 - k$

9. ___{41}___

10. It is the square of 2, 3, or 4.

10. ___{4, 9, 16}___

Write an open sentence for each solution set.

11. {A, E, I, O, U}

11. ___It is a vowel.___

12. {1, 3, 5, 7, 9}

12. ___It is an odd number between 0 and 10.___

13. {June, July, August}

13. ___It is a summer month.___

14. {Atlantic, Pacific, Indian, Arctic}

14. ___It is an ocean.___

Enrichment

Equivalent Sets

Two sets are **equal,** or identical, if they contain exactly the
same elements. The order in which we name the elements is
unimportant. Thus, {a, b, c, d} and {c, a, d, b} are equal sets. Two
sets are **equivalent** if for every element of one set there is one
and only one element in the other set; that is, there exists a
one-to-one matching between the elements of the two sets. The
one-to-one matchings below show that the sets are equivalent.

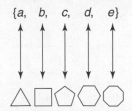

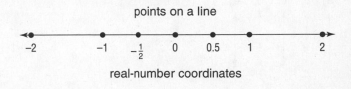

Consider these equivalent sets.
Set of whole numbers =
{0, 1, 2, 3, 4, 5, ⋯}

Set of even whole numbers =
{0, 2, 4, 6, 8, 10, ⋯}

Are there more whole numbers or more even whole numbers? Or
might there be the same number of each, even though we have no
counting number to tell how many?

A one-to-one matching of the whole
numbers and the even whole numbers
appears at the right. Each whole number n
is matched with the even number $2n$, and
each even number $2n$ is matched with the
whole number n. Therefore, the two sets are equivalent. This
means that there are as many even whole numbers as there are
whole numbers.

$$\{0, 1, 2, 3, 4, 5, \cdots, n, \cdots\}$$
$$\{0, 2, 4, 6, 8, 10, \cdots, 2n, \cdots\}$$

**Use a one-to-one matching to show that the two
sets are equivalent.**

1. {Amy, Betsy, Carol, Dorothy} and {Al, Bob, Carl, David} _____

2. {1, 2, 3, 4, 5, ⋯} and {3, 6, 9, 12, 15, ⋯} _____

3. {−1, −2, −3, −4, ⋯} and {1, 2, 3, 4, ⋯} _____

4. {1, 2, 3, 4, 5, ⋯} and {1, 3, 5, 7, 9, ⋯} _____

NAME _____ DATE _____ PERIOD _____

Enrichment

Equivalent Sets

Two sets are **equal,** or identical, if they contain exactly the
same elements. The order in which we name the elements is
unimportant. Thus, {*a, b, c, d*} and {*c, a, d, b*} are equal sets. Two
sets are **equivalent** if for every element of one set there is one
and only one element in the other set; that is, there exists a
one-to-one matching between the elements of the two sets. The
one-to-one matchings below show that the sets are equivalent.

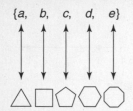

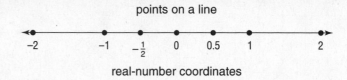

points on a line

real-number coordinates

Consider these equivalent sets.

Set of whole numbers =
{0, 1, 2, 3, 4, 5, ···}

Set of even whole numbers =
{0, 2, 4, 6, 8, 10, ···}

Are there more whole numbers or more even whole numbers? Or
might there be the same number of each, even though we have no
counting number to tell how many?

A one-to-one matching of the whole
numbers and the even whole numbers
appears at the right. Each whole number n
is matched with the even number $2n$, and
each even number $2n$ is matched with the
whole number n. Therefore, the two sets are equivalent. This
means that there are as many even whole numbers as there are
whole numbers.

$$\{0, 1, 2, 3, 4, 5, \cdots, n, \cdots\}$$
$$\updownarrow \updownarrow \updownarrow \updownarrow \updownarrow \updownarrow \qquad \searrow$$
$$\{0, 2, 4, 6, 8, 10, \cdots, 2n, \cdots\}$$

Use a one-to-one matching to show that the two sets are equivalent.

1. {Amy, Betsy, Carol, Dorothy} and {Al, Bob, Carl, David}

$$\textbf{\{Amy, Betsy, Carol, Dorothy\}}$$
$$\updownarrow \qquad \updownarrow \qquad \updownarrow \qquad \updownarrow$$
$$\underline{\textbf{\{ Al, \quad Bob, \quad Carl, \quad David \}}}$$

2. {1, 2, 3, 4, 5, ···} and {3, 6, 9, 12, 15, ···}

$$\textbf{\{1, 2, 3, 4, 5, \cdots\}}$$
$$\updownarrow \updownarrow \updownarrow \updownarrow \updownarrow$$
$$\underline{\textbf{\{3, 6, 9, 12, 15, \cdots\}}}$$

3. {−1, −2, −3, −4, ···} and {1, 2, 3, 4, ···}

$$\textbf{\{-1, -2, -3, -4, \cdots\}}$$
$$\updownarrow \quad \updownarrow \quad \updownarrow \quad \updownarrow$$
$$\underline{\textbf{\{ 1, \quad 2, \quad 3, \quad 4, \cdots\}}}$$

4. {1, 2, 3, 4, 5, ···} and {1, 3, 5, 7, 9, ···}

$$\textbf{\{1, 2, 3, 4, 5, \cdots\}}$$
$$\updownarrow \updownarrow \updownarrow \updownarrow \updownarrow$$
$$\underline{\textbf{\{1, 3, 5, 7, 9, \cdots\}}}$$

3-6

Enrichment

Conditional Statements

If p and q represent statements, the compound statement "if p then q" is called a **conditional**.

symbol: $p \rightarrow q$ read: either "if p then q" or "p only if q"

The statement p is called the **antecedent**, and the statement q is called the **consequent**.

For each conditional statement identify the antecedent (A) and the consequent (C).

1. If it is nine o'clock, then I am late.

   A: _____

   C: _____

2. If Karen is home, then we will ask her to come.

   A: _____

   C: _____

3. The fish will die if we don't feed them.

   A: _____

   C: _____

4. There will be no school if it snows.

   A: _____

   C: _____

5. There will be no school only if it snows.

   A: _____

   C: _____

6. If $y + 2 = 6$ then $y = 4$.

   A: _____

   C: _____

19   *Algebra: Concepts and Applications*

Enrichment

Conditional Statements

If p and q represent statements, the compound statement "if p then q" is called a **conditional**.

symbol: $p \rightarrow q$ read: either "if p then q" or "p only if q"

The statement p is called the **antecedent**, and the statement q is called the **consequent**.

For each conditional statement identify the antecedent (A) and the consequent (C).

1. If it is nine o'clock, then I am late.

   A: **It is 9:00.**

   C: **I am late.**

2. If Karen is home, then we will ask her to come.

   A: **Karen is home.**

   C: **We will ask Karen to come.**

3. The fish will die if we don't feed them.

   A: **We don't feed the fish.**

   C: **The fish will die.**

4. There will be no school if it snows.

   A: **It snows, or it is snowing.**

   C: **There will be no school.**

5. There will be no school only if it snows.

   A: **There will be no school.**

   C: **It is snowing.**

6. If $y + 2 = 6$ then $y = 4$.

   A: **$y + 2 = 6$**

   C: **$y = 4$**

3-7

Enrichment

Distance on the Number Line

The **absolute value** of the difference between two integers can be interpreted as the distance between two points on a number line. That is, if point A has a as a coordinate and point B has b as a coordinate, then $|a - b|$ is the distance between points A and B.

Graph each pair of points on the number line. Then write an expression using absolute value to find the distance between the points.

1. H at -4 and G at 2

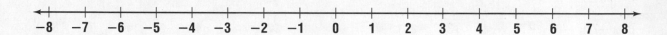

2. X at -7 and Y at -1

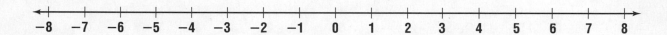

3. A at 5 and B at -5

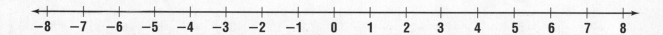

Use the number lines to solve the problems.

4. Graph two points, M and N, that are each 5 units from -2. Make $M > N$.

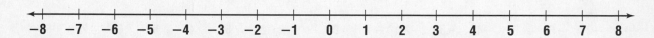

5. Graph the two solutions to the equation $|y - 2| = 3$. Call the points y_1 and y_2.

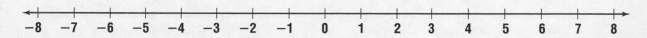

Algebra: Concepts and Applications

Enrichment

Distance on the Number Line

The **absolute value** of the difference between two integers can be interpreted as the distance between two points on a number line. That is, if point A has a as a coordinate and point B has b as a coordinate, then $|a - b|$ is the distance between points A and B.

Graph each pair of points on the number line. Then write an expression using absolute value to find the distance between the points.

1. H at -4 and G at 2 $|(-4) - 2| = 6$

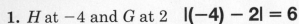

2. X at -7 and Y at -1 $|(-7) - (-1)| = 6$

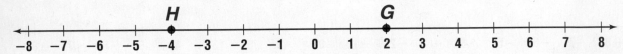

3. A at 5 and B at -5 $|5 - (-5)| = 10$

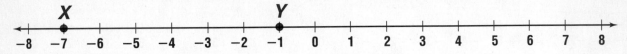

Use the number lines to solve the problems.

4. Graph two points, M and N, that are each 5 units from -2. Make $M > N$.

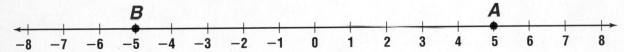

5. Graph the two solutions to the equation $|y - 2| = 3$. Call the points y_1 and y_2.

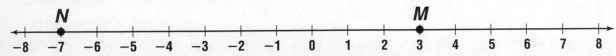

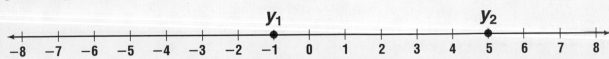

4-1

Enrichment

Density of Rational Numbers

Shown below is a portion of the number line containing all points from 0 to $\frac{1}{4}$. The coordinate of point F is $\frac{1}{8}$, which is half of $\frac{1}{4}$.

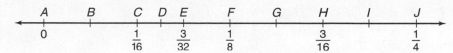

The coordinate of point C is $\frac{1}{16}$, which is half of $\frac{1}{8}$.

Between any two rational numbers, there is an unlimited number of other rational numbers. This property is called the **density property** of rational numbers.

M   N   O   P   Q

$\frac{3}{5}$ $\frac{13}{20}$ $\frac{4}{5}$

$$\frac{13}{20} > \frac{3}{5} \text{ and } \frac{13}{20} < \frac{4}{5}$$

The easiest point to locate between two given points is the point halfway between those two points. This point is half the sum of the two coordinates.

V   W   X   Y   Z

$\frac{7}{16}$ $\frac{8}{16}$

$$\frac{1}{2}\left(\frac{7}{16} + \frac{8}{16}\right) \rightarrow \frac{1}{2}\left(\frac{15}{16}\right) \rightarrow \frac{15}{32}$$

The coordinate of point X is $\frac{15}{32}$.

Using the number lines above, state the coordinates of each point. Assume that each point is halfway between the points to the left and right.

1. B 2. D 3. G 4. I

5. O 6. P 7. W 8. Y

Name the rational number that is halfway between the two given numbers on a number line.

9. $\frac{1}{2}$ and $\frac{3}{4}$ 10. 0 and 5   11. 4 and $5\frac{1}{4}$

12. $1\frac{1}{2}$ and $\frac{5}{8}$ 13. $\frac{1}{2}$ and $\frac{2}{3}$ 14. $\frac{7}{8}$ and $\frac{8}{9}$

Density of Rational Numbers

Shown below is a portion of the number line containing all points from 0 to $\frac{1}{4}$. The coordinate of point F is $\frac{1}{8}$, which is half of $\frac{1}{4}$.

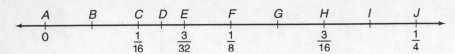

The coordinate of point C is $\frac{1}{16}$, which is half of $\frac{1}{8}$.

Between any two rational numbers, there is an unlimited number of other rational numbers. This property is called the **density property** of rational numbers.

$$\frac{13}{20} > \frac{3}{5} \text{ and } \frac{13}{20} < \frac{4}{5}$$

The easiest point to locate between two given points is the point halfway between those two points. This point is half the sum of the two coordinates.

$$\frac{1}{2}\left(\frac{7}{16} + \frac{8}{16}\right) \rightarrow \frac{1}{2}\left(\frac{15}{16}\right) \rightarrow \frac{15}{32}$$

The coordinate of point X is $\frac{15}{32}$.

Using the number lines above, state the coordinates of each point. Assume that each point is halfway between the points to the left and right.

1. B $\dfrac{1}{32}$

2. D $\dfrac{5}{64}$

3. G $\dfrac{5}{32}$

4. I $\dfrac{7}{32}$

5. O $\dfrac{7}{10}$

6. P $\dfrac{3}{4}$

7. W $\dfrac{29}{64}$

8. Y $\dfrac{31}{64}$

Name the rational number that is halfway between the two given numbers on a number line.

9. $\frac{1}{2}$ and $\frac{3}{4}$ $\dfrac{5}{8}$

10. 0 and 5 $2\dfrac{1}{2}$

11. 4 and $5\frac{1}{4}$ $4\dfrac{5}{8}$

12. $1\frac{1}{2}$ and $\frac{5}{8}$ $1\dfrac{1}{16}$

13. $\frac{1}{2}$ and $\frac{2}{3}$ $\dfrac{7}{12}$

14. $\frac{7}{8}$ and $\frac{8}{9}$ $\dfrac{127}{144}$

4-2

Enrichment

Outcomes

Complete.

1. Complete the spinner so that it will have six different possible outcomes.

2. List the numbers that could be placed on the die to provide only four different possible outcomes.

3. Complete the spinner so that it is more likely to land on red than blue.

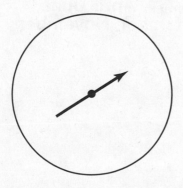

4. List the months in which you could choose a date and have 30 possible outcomes.

5. There are white, green, and blue marbles in a bag. What is the minimum number of each so that it is twice as likely that you draw a green one as a white one, and three times as likely that you draw a blue one as a green one?

6. A year between 1950 and 2001 is chosen at random. How many possible outcomes are there where the year is a leap year? List them.

Algebra: Concepts and Applications

Outcomes

Complete.

1. Complete the spinner so that it will have six different possible outcomes.

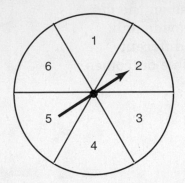

The six sections do not have to be the same size.

2. List the numbers that could be placed on the die to provide only four different possible outcomes. **Sample answer: 1, 1, 1, 2, 3, 4**

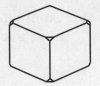

3. Complete the spinner so that it is more likely to land on red than blue.

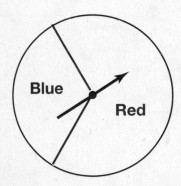

Red section must be larger than blue section.

4. List the months in which you could choose a date and have 30 possible outcomes. **April, June, September, November**

5. There are white, green, and blue marbles in a bag. What is the minimum number of each so that it is twice as likely that you draw a green one as a white one, and three times as likely that you draw a blue one as a green one? **1 white, 2 green, and 6 blue**

6. A year between 1950 and 2001 is chosen at random. How many possible outcomes are there where the year is a leap year? List them. **13 outcomes; 1952, 1956, 1960, 1964, 1968, 1972, 1976, 1980, 1984, 1988, 1992, 1996, 2000**

Student Edition
Pages 154–159

4-3

Enrichment

Decimal Hunt

Each of the sentences below is missing two parts, an operation symbol (+ , − , × , ÷) and a result. The missing results are given in the box at the right. Use guess and check to find the operations and the results that make each sentence true.

1. 12.35 ◯ 4.16 = [_____]

2. 6.25 ◯ 3.06 = [_____]

3. 38.052 ◯ 12.6 = [_____]

4. 0.08 ◯ 2.5 = [_____]

5. 21.45 ◯ 13.237 = [_____]

6. 1.987 ◯ 1.025 = [_____]

7. 7.23 ◯ 8.669 = [_____]

8. 30.68 ◯ 12.228 = [_____]

9. 8.35 ◯ 3.24 = [_____]

10. 2.3625 ◯ 1.35 = [_____]

0.032
1.75
2.036675
3.02
8.213
9.31
15.899
18.452
27.054
51.376

Decimal Hunt

Each of the sentences below is missing two parts, an operation symbol (+ , − , × , ÷) and a result. The missing results are given in the box at the right. Use guess and check to find the operations and the results that make each sentence true.

1. 12.35 ⊗ 4.16 = | **51.376** |

2. 6.25 ⊕ 3.06 = | **9.31** |

3. 38.052 ⊘ 12.6 = | **3.02** |

4. 0.08 ⊘ 2.5 = | **0.032** |

5. 21.45 ⊖ 13.237 = | **8.213** |

6. 1.987 ⊗ 1.025 = | **2.036675** |

7. 7.23 ⊕ 8.669 = | **15.899** |

8. 30.68 ⊖ 12.228 = | **18.452** |

9. 8.35 ⊗ 3.24 = | **27.054** |

10. 2.3625 ⊘ 1.35 = | **1.75** |

0.032
1.75
2.036675
3.02
8.213
9.31
15.899
18.452
27.054
51.376

T23 *Algebra: Concepts and Applications*

NAME _____ DATE _____ PERIOD _____

Enrichment

Student Edition
Pages 160–164

Puzzle

Solve each equation. The first one is completed.

1. $\dfrac{m}{12} = 13$

2. $17v = -578$

3. $\dfrac{c}{75} = 18$

4. $-252d = -5796$

5. $64 \cdot w = 5568$

6. $g \div 29 = 61$

7. $p(85) = -7225$

8. $39x = 663$

9. $\dfrac{k}{18} = 30$

10. $\dfrac{z}{-94} = -32$

11. $-112q = 1456$

12. $201y = -1608$

1. ___156___ U

2. _____ E

3. _____ R

4. _____ H

5. _____ O

6. _____ B

7. _____ T

8. _____ I

9. _____ A

10. _____ N

11. _____ F

12. _____ S

Put the letter that is next to each solution in the box below the corresponding solution shown above.

What is a RINGLEADER?

-85	23	-34		-13	17	1350	-8	-85		87	3008	-34

17	3008		-85	23	-34		1769	540	-85	23	-85	156	1769

Puzzle

Solve each equation. The first one is completed.

1. $\frac{m}{12} = 13$

2. $17v = -578$

3. $\frac{c}{75} = 18$

4. $-252d = -5796$

5. $64 \cdot w = 5568$

6. $g \div 29 = 61$

7. $p(85) = -7225$

8. $39x = 663$

9. $\frac{k}{18} = 30$

10. $\frac{z}{-94} = -32$

11. $-112q = 1456$

12. $201y = -1608$

1. _____156_____ U

2. _____−34_____ E

3. _____1350_____ R

4. _____23_____ H

5. _____87_____ O

6. _____1769_____ B

7. _____−85_____ T

8. _____17_____ I

9. _____540_____ A

10. _____3008_____ N

11. _____−13_____ F

12. _____−8_____ S

Put the letter that is next to each solution in the box below the corresponding solution shown above.

What is a RINGLEADER?

−85	23	−34		−13	17	1350	−8	−85		87	3008	−34
T	H	E		F	I	R	S	T		O	N	E

17	3008		−85	23	−34		1769	540	−85	23	−85	156	1769
I	N		T	H	E		B	A	T	H	T	U	B

Equations With No Solutions

Not every equation has a solution. Watch what happens when
we try to solve the following equation.

$$8 - (3 - 2x) = 5x - 3x$$
$$8 - 3 + 2x = 2x$$
$$5 + 2x = 2x$$
$$5 = 0$$

Since the equation is equivalent to the false statement $5 = 0$, it
has no solution. There is no value of x that will make the
equation true.

**Write a false statement that shows each equation has no
solution.**

1. $1 - 2t = 2(1 - t)$

2. $11y - 7y = 5 + 4y - 6$

3. $-7x^2 + 5 + 6x^2 = 12 - (2 + x^2)$

4. $2(2 - y^2) = 5 - (5 + 2y^2)$

5. $\frac{3}{2} + \frac{2}{3}p - 1 = \frac{1}{3}(1 + 2p)$

6. $0.5(1 + 3m) = 1.05 - (1 - 1.5m)$

Solve each equation if possible.

7. $5(3 - m) = 15m + 15$

8. $-9x + 12x = 3(2 - x)$

9. $10(0.2 + 0.4c) = 10c + 0.2 - 6c$

10. $13 - (3 - n) = 5(n + 2)$

11. $2(1 + 4t) = 8 - (3 - 8t)$

12. $3(d - 1) + 2 = 3(d + 2) - 5$

4-5

Enrichment

Equations With No Solutions

Not every equation has a solution. Watch what happens when
we try to solve the following equation.

$$8 - (3 - 2x) = 5x - 3x$$
$$8 - 3 + 2x = 2x$$
$$5 + 2x = 2x$$
$$5 = 0$$

Since the equation is equivalent to the false statement $5 = 0$, it
has no solution. There is no value of x that will make the
equation true.

**Write a false statement that shows each equation has no
solution. Sample answers are given.**

1. $1 - 2t = 2(1 - t)$
1 = 2

2. $11y - 7y = 5 + 4y - 6$
0 = −1

3. $-7x^2 + 5 + 6x^2 = 12 - (2 + x^2)$
5 = 10

4. $2(2 - y^2) = 5 - (5 + 2y^2)$
4 = 0

5. $\frac{3}{2} + \frac{2}{3}p - 1 = \frac{1}{3}(1 + 2p)$
$\frac{1}{2} = \frac{1}{3}$

6. $0.5(1 + 3m) = 1.05 - (1 - 1.5m)$
0.5 = 0.05

Solve each equation if possible.

7. $5(3 - m) = 15m + 15$
m = 0

8. $-9x + 12x = 3(2 - x)$
x = 1

9. $10(0.2 + 0.4c) = 10c + 0.2 - 6c$
no solution

10. $13 - (3 - n) = 5(n + 2)$
n = 0

11. $2(1 + 4t) = 8 - (3 - 8t)$
no solution

12. $3(d - 1) + 2 = 3(d + 2) - 5$
no solution

Identities

Any equation that is true for every value of the variable is called an **identity.** When you try to solve an identity, you end up with a statement that is always true. Here is an example.

$$8 - (5 - 6x) = 3(1 + 2x)$$
$$8 - 5 + 6x = 3 + 6x$$
$$3 + 6x = 3 + 6x$$

State whether each equation is an identity. If it is not, find its solution.

1. $2(2 - 3x) = 3(3 + x) + 4$

2. $5(m + 1) + 6 = 3(4 + m) + (2m - 1)$

3. $(5t + 9) - (3t - 13) = 2(11 + t)$

4. $14 - (6 - 3c) = 4c - c$

5. $3y - 2(y + 19) = 9y - 3(9 - y)$

6. $3(3h - 1) = 4(h + 3)$

7. Start with the true statement $3x - 2 = 3x - 2$. Use it to create an identity of your own.

8. Start with the false statement $1 = 2$. Use it to create an equation with no solution.

Identities

Any equation that is true for every value of the variable is
called an **identity.** When you try to solve an identity, you end
up with a statement that is always true. Here is an example.

$$8 - (5 - 6x) = 3(1 + 2x)$$

$$8 - 5 + 6x = 3 + 6x$$

$$3 + 6x = 3 + 6x$$

**State whether each equation is an identity. If it is not, find its
solution.**

1. $2(2 - 3x) = 3(3 + x) + 4$
$x = -1$

2. $5(m + 1) + 6 = 3(4 + m) + (2m - 1)$
identity

3. $(5t + 9) - (3t - 13) = 2(11 + t)$
identity

4. $14 - (6 - 3c) = 4c - c$
no solution

5. $3y - 2(y + 19) = 9y - 3(9 - y)$
$y = -1$

6. $3(3h - 1) = 4(h + 3)$
$h = 3$

7. Start with the true statement $3x - 2 = 3x - 2$. Use it to
create an identity of your own. **See students' work.**

8. Start with the false statement $1 = 2$. Use it to create an
equation with no solution. **See students' work.**

Enrichment

Using Equations

Use what you have learned about equations to solve each problem.

1. In many universities, grade point averages are figured out using a table like this.

grade	A	B	C	D	F
point value	4	3	2	1	0

Different classes often meet for a different number of hours each week. If you had the following schedule and grades, your average would be 2.45.

Course	Hours	Grade
Chemistry	3	C
Chemistry Lab	2	F
Calculus	5	A
Phys. Ed.	1	C
Total	11	

$$\frac{3(2) + 2(0) + 5(4) + 1(2)}{11} = \frac{28}{11} = 2.54$$

Suppose you are taking the following courses and you know all your grades but your math grade. What is the lowest math grade you could receive and still have a grade point average of over 3.00?

Course	Hours	Grade
Biology	5	A
Spanish	3	B
Math	4	?
English	4	B
Phys. Ed.	1	D
Total	17	

2. Read the information below the soccer standings at the right to understand how a team's points are determined. A shootout is a form of tie-breaker used when the score is still tied after an overtime period.

   a. A team had 5 wins, 2 shootout victories and 23 bonus points. Show that the number of points must be 61.

   b. To find the number of shootout victories for Golden Bay, let x = number of shootout victories. Then, $5 - x$ = number of regulation or overtime wins.
   $$6(5 - x) + 4x + 32 = 60$$
   Solve this equation.

   c. Find the number of shootout victories for Chicago.

Soccer

NASL

Eastern Division	W	L	GF	GA	BP	Pts.
Chicago	10	9	42	40	42	94
Cosmos	10	6	31	27	29	89
Toronto	8	8	33	22	29	71
Tampa Bay	7	12	31	49	27	67

Western Division	W	L	GF	GA	BP	Pts.
Vancouver	11	6	39	33	32	96
Minnesota	10	6	30	30	26	82
San Diego	9	9	33	38	27	75
Tulsa	7	10	31	32	29	71
Golden Bay	5	11	43	42	32	60

Six points are awarded for a regulation or overtime win, four points for a shootout victory, and one bonus point for every goal scored with a maximum of three per game. No bonus point is awarded for overtime or shootout goals.

4-7

Enrichment

Using Equations

Use what you have learned about equations to solve each problem.

1. In many universities, grade point averages are figured out using a table like this.

grade	A	B	C	D	F
point value	4	3	2	1	0

Different classes often meet for a different number of hours each week. If you had the following schedule and grades, your average would be 2.45.

Course	Hours	Grade
Chemistry	3	C
Chemistry Lab	2	F
Calculus	5	A
Phys. Ed.	1	C
Total	11	

$$\frac{3(2) + 2(0) + 5(4) + 1(2)}{11} = \frac{28}{11} = 2.54$$

Suppose you are taking the following courses and you know all your grades but your math grade. What is the lowest math grade you could receive and still have a grade point average of over 3.00? **B**

Course	Hours	Grade
Biology	5	A
Spanish	3	B
Math	4	?
English	4	B
Phys. Ed.	1	D
Total	17	

2. Read the information below the soccer standings at the right to understand how a team's points are determined. A shootout is a form of tie-breaker used when the score is still tied after an overtime period.

a. A team had 5 wins, 2 shootout victories and 23 bonus points. Show that the number of points must be 61.

$$6(5) + 4(2) + 23 = 61$$

b. To find the number of shootout victories for Golden Bay, let x = number of shootout victories. Then, $5 - x$ = number of regulation or overtime wins. $30 - 6x + 4x + 32 = 60$

$$6(5 - x) + 4x + 32 = 60 \qquad -2x = -2$$
$$x = 1$$

Solve this equation.

c. Find the number of shootout victories for Chicago.

$$6(10 - x) + 4x + 42 = 94$$
$$60 - 6x + 4x + 42 = 94$$
$$-2x = -8$$
$$x = 4$$

Soccer

NASL

Eastern Division	W	L	GF	GA	BP	Pts.
Chicago	10	9	42	40	42	94
Cosmos	10	6	31	27	29	89
Toronto	8	8	33	22	29	71
Tampa Bay	7	12	31	49	27	67

Western Division	W	L	GF	GA	BP	Pts.
Vancouver	11	6	39	33	32	96
Minnesota	10	6	30	30	26	82
San Diego	9	9	33	38	27	75
Tulsa	7	10	31	32	29	71
Golden Bay	5	11	43	42	32	60

Six points are awarded for a regulation or overtime win, four points for a shootout victory, and one bonus point for every goal scored with a maximum of three per game. No bonus point is awarded for overtime or shootout goals.

5-1

Enrichment

Scale Drawings

The map at the left below shows building lots for sale. The scale ratio is 1:2400. At the right below is the floor plan for a two-bedroom apartment. The length of the living room is 6 m. On the plan the living room is 6 cm long.

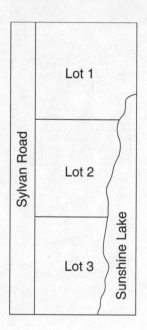

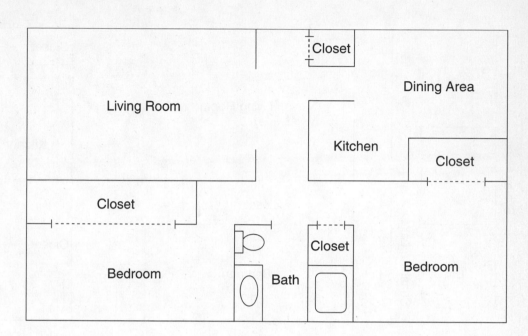

Answer each question.

1. On the map, how many feet are represented by an inch?

2. On the map, measure the frontage of Lot 2 on Sylvan Road in inches. What is the actual frontage in feet?

3. What is the scale ratio represented on the floor plan?

4. On the floor plan, measure the width of the living room in centimeters. What is the actual width in meters?

5. About how many square meters of carpeting would be needed to carpet the living room?

6. Make a scale drawing of your classroom using an appropriate scale.

7. On the scale for a map of Lancaster, Pennsylvania, 2.5 cm equals 3 km. Find the scale ratio.

5-1 Enrichment

Student Edition
Pages 188–193

Scale Drawings

The map at the left below shows building lots for sale. The scale ratio is 1:2400. At the right below is the floor plan for a two-, bedroom apartment. The length of the living room is 6 m. On the plan the living room is 6 cm long.

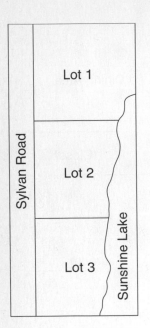

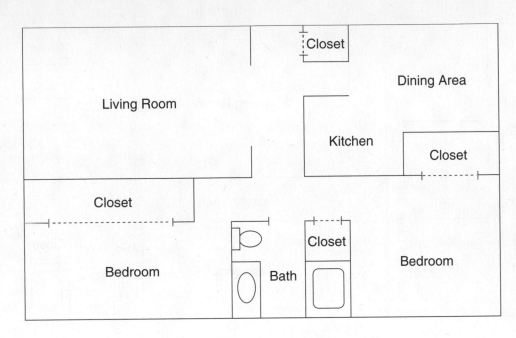

Answer each question.

1. On the map, how many feet are represented by an inch? **200 ft**

2. On the map, measure the frontage of Lot 2 on Sylvan Road in inches. What is the actual frontage in feet? **200 ft**

3. What is the scale ratio represented on the floor plan? **1:100**

4. On the floor plan, measure the width of the living room in centimeters. What is the actual width in meters? **4 m**

5. About how many square meters of carpeting would be needed to carpet the living room? **24 m²**

6. Make a scale drawing of your classroom using an appropriate scale. **See students' work.**

7. On the scale for a map of Lancaster, Pennsylvania, 2.5 cm equals 3 km. Find the scale ratio. **1:120,000**

5-2

Enrichment

Growth Charts

Graphs are often used by doctors to show parents the growth rates of their children. The horizontal scale of the chart at the right shows the ages from 15 to 36 months. The vertical scale shows weight in kilograms. One kilogram is about 2.2 pounds. The curved lines are used to show how a child's weight compares with others of his or her age.

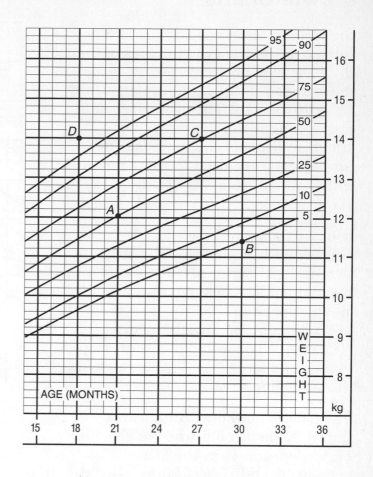

Look at the point labeled *A*. It represents a 21-month-old who weighs 12 kilograms. It is located on the slanted line labeled 50. This means the child's weight is in the "50th percentile." In other words, 50% of all 21-month-olds weigh more than 12 kilograms and 50% weigh less than 12 kilograms.

The location of Point *B* indicates that a 30-month-old who weighs 11.4 kilograms is in the 5th percentile. Only 5% of 30-month-old children will weigh less than 11.4 kilograms.

Solve.

1. Look at the point labeled *C*. How much does the child weigh? How old is he? What percent of children his age will weigh more than he does?

2. Look at the point labeled *D*. What is the child's age and weight? What percent of children her age will weigh more than she does?

3. What is the 50th percentile weight for a child 27 months old?

4. How much weight would child *B* have to gain to be in the 50th percentile?

5. If child *D* did not gain any weight for four months, what percentile would he be in?

6. How much heavier is a $2\frac{1}{2}$-year-old in the 90th percentile than one in the 10th percentile?

Algebra: Concepts and Applications

Enrichment

Growth Charts

Graphs are often used by doctors to show parents the growth rates of their children. The horizontal scale of the chart at the right shows the ages from 15 to 36 months. The vertical scale shows weight in kilograms. One kilogram is about 2.2 pounds. The curved lines are used to show how a child's weight compares with others of his or her age.

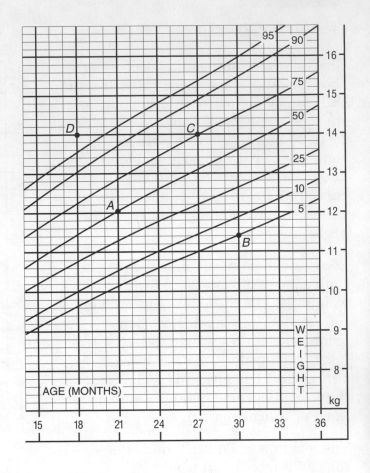

Look at the point labeled *A*. It represents a 21-month-old who weighs 12 kilograms. It is located on the slanted line labeled 50. This means the child's weight is in the "50th percentile." In other words, 50% of all 21-month-olds weigh more than 12 kilograms and 50% weigh less than 12 kilograms.

The location of Point *B* indicates that a 30-month-old who weighs 11.4 kilograms is in the 5th percentile. Only 5% of 30-month-old children will weigh less than 11.4 kilograms.

Solve.

1. Look at the point labeled *C*. How much does the child weigh? How old is he? What percent of children his age will weigh more than he does? **14 kg; 27 months; 25%**

2. Look at the point labeled *D*. What is the child's age and weight? What percent of children her age will weigh more than she does? **18 months; 14 kg; less than 5%**

3. What is the 50th percentile weight for a child 27 months old? **13.1 kg**

4. How much weight would child *B* have to gain to be in the 50th percentile? **2.2 kg**

5. If child *D* did not gain any weight for four months, what percentile would he be in? **90th**

6. How much heavier is a $2\frac{1}{2}$-year-old in the 90th percentile than one in the 10th percentile? **3.6 kg**

NAME _____ DATE _____ PERIOD _____

Enrichment

Partnerships

Two or more people who agree to combine their money, goods, or skill in some business often do so by forming a *partnership*. Gains and losses in a partnership are usually divided in proportion to the amount of money each person has invested.

Sharon and Tina start a business to print restaurant menus using Tina's computer. For supplies and software, Sharon invests $1200 and Tina, $800. If their profit after the first year is $500, what is each person's share?

The entire investment is $1200 plus $800, or $2000.

Sharon's share is $\frac{\$1200}{\$2238}$, or $\frac{3}{5}$. Tina's share is $\frac{\$800}{\$2238}$, or $\frac{2}{5}$.

Answer each question.

1. In the problem above, what is Sharon's share of the profit?

2. What is Tina's share?

3. Sal and Mario were partners in a construction business. Sal put in $5238 and Mario, $4238. Their profit in 3 years was $4500. What was each partner's share?

4. Tim, Bob, and Alice entered into a business partnership for 2 years. Tim put in $3600, Bob put in $2400, and Alice put in $2238. If their profit was $3238, what was each person's share?

5. Fred, Vito, and Hal began with a capital of $28,238. Fred furnished $7238; Vito, $6238; and Hal, the remainder. If they gained 14% on their investment, what was each person's share?

6. A storeroom belonging to Taylor, Bartinelli, & Wong was entirely destroyed by fire. They received $9675 insurance. What was each person's share, if Taylor owned 15%, Bartinelli, 40%, and Wong the remainder?

7. Divide a profit of $7200 between two partners so that the ratio of the shares is 4 to 5.

8. Divide a profit of $18,238 among three partners so that the ratio of the shares is 1:2:3.

Algebra: Concepts and Applications

5-3

Enrichment

Partnerships

Two or more people who agree to combine their money, goods, or skill in some business often do so by forming a *partnership*. Gains and losses in a partnership are usually divided in proportion to the amount of money each person has invested.

Sharon and Tina start a business to print restaurant menus using Tina's computer. For supplies and software, Sharon invests $1200 and Tina, $800. If their profit after the first year is $500, what is each person's share?

The entire investment is $1200 plus $800, or $2000.

Sharon's share is $\frac{\$1200}{\$2238}$, or $\frac{3}{5}$. Tina's share is $\frac{\$800}{\$2238}$, or $\frac{2}{5}$.

Answer each question.

1. In the problem above, what is Sharon's share of the profit? **$300**

2. What is Tina's share? **$200**

3. Sal and Mario were partners in a construction business. Sal put in $5238 and Mario, $4238. Their profit in 3 years was $4500. What was each partner's share?
Sal: $2500; Mario: $2238

4. Tim, Bob, and Alice entered into a business partnership for 2 years. Tim put in $3600, Bob put in $2400, and Alice put in $2238. If their profit was $3238, what was each person's share?
Tim: $1350; Bob: $900; Alice: $750

5. Fred, Vito, and Hal began with a capital of $28,238. Fred furnished $7238; Vito, $6238; and Hal, the remainder. If they gained 14% on their investment, what was each person's share? **Fred: $980; Vito: $840; Hal: $2100**

6. A storeroom belonging to Taylor, Bartinelli, & Wong was entirely destroyed by fire. They received $9675 insurance. What was each person's share, if Taylor owned 15%, Bartinelli, 40%, and Wong the remainder?
Taylor: $1451.25; Bartinelli: $3870; Wong: $4353.75

7. Divide a profit of $7200 between two partners so that the ratio of the shares is 4 to 5. **$3200, $4238**

8. Divide a profit of $18,238 among three partners so that the ratio of the shares is 1:2:3. **$3238, $6238, $9238**

Using Percent

Use what you have learned about percent to solve each problem.

A TV movie had a "rating" of 15 and a 25 "share." The rating of 15 means that 15% of the nation's total TV households were tuned in to this show. The 25 share means that 25% of the homes with TVs turned on were tuned to the movie. How many TV households had their TVs turned off at this time?

To find out, let T = the number of TV households
and x = the number of TV households with the TV off.
Then $T - x$ = the number of TV households with the TV on.

Since $0.15T$ and $0.25(T - x)$ both represent the number of households tuned to the movie,

$$0.15T = 0.25(T - x)$$
$$0.15T = 0.25T - 0.25x.$$

Solve for x.
$$0.25x = 0.10T$$
$$x = \frac{0.10T}{0.25} = 0.40T$$

Forty percent of the TV households had their TVs off when the movie was aired.

Answer each question.

1. During that same week, a sports broadcast had a rating of 22.1 and a 43 share. Show that the percent of TV households with their TVs off was about 48.6%.

2. Find the percent of TV households with their TVs turned off during a show with a rating of 18.9 and a 29 share.

3. Show that if T is the number of TV households, r is the rating, and s is the share, then the number of TV households with the TV off is $\frac{(s - r)T}{s}$.

4. If the fraction of TV households with no TV on is $\frac{s - r}{s}$ then show that the fraction of TV households with TVs on is $\frac{r}{s}$.

5. Find the percent of TV households with TVs on during the most watched serial program in history: the last episode of *M*A*S*H,* which had a 60.3 rating and a 77 share.

6. A local station now has a 2 share. Each share is worth $50,000 in advertising revenue per month. The station is thinking of going commercial free for the three months of summer to gain more listeners. What would its new share have to be for the last 4 months of the year to make more money for the year than it would have made had it not gone commercial free?

NAME _____ DATE _____ PERIOD _____

Enrichment

Using Percent

Use what you have learned about percent to solve each problem.

A TV movie had a "rating" of 15 and a 25 "share." The rating of 15 means that 15% of the nation's total TV households were tuned in to this show. The 25 share means that 25% of the homes with TVs turned on were tuned to the movie. How many TV households had their TVs turned off at this time?

To find out, let T = the number of TV households
and x = the number of TV households with the TV off.
Then $T - x$ = the number of TV households with the TV on.

Since $0.15T$ and $0.25(T - x)$ both represent the number of households tuned to the movie,

$$0.15T = 0.25(T - x)$$
$$0.15T = 0.25T - 0.25x.$$

Solve for x.
$$0.25x = 0.10T$$
$$x = \frac{0.10T}{0.25} = 0.40T$$

Forty percent of the TV households had their TVs off when the movie was aired.

Answer each question.

1. During that same week, a sports broadcast had a rating of 22.1 and a 43 share. Show that the percent of TV households with their TVs off was about 48.6%.

$$0.221T = 0.43T - 0.43x$$
$$x = \frac{0.221T - 0.43T}{-0.43}$$
$$= 0.486T$$

2. Find the percent of TV households with their TVs turned off during a show with a rating of 18.9 and a 29 share. **34.8%**

3. Show that if T is the number of TV households, r is the rating, and s is the share, then the number of TV households with the TV off is $\frac{(s - r)T}{s}$. **Solve $rT = s(T - x)$ for x.**

4. If the fraction of TV households with no TV on is $\frac{s - r}{s}$ then show that the fraction of TV households with TVs on is $\frac{r}{s}$. $1 - \frac{s - r}{s} = \frac{r}{s}$

5. Find the percent of TV households with TVs on during the most watched serial program in history: the last episode of *M*A*S*H*, which had a 60.3 rating and a 77 share. $\frac{60.3}{77} = 78.3\%$

6. A local station now has a 2 share. Each share is worth $50,000 in advertising revenue per month. The station is thinking of going commercial free for the three months of summer to gain more listeners. What would its new share have to be for the last 4 months of the year to make more money for the year than it would have made had it not gone commercial free? **greater than 3.5**

5-5

Enrichment

Compound Interest

In most banks, interest on savings accounts is compounded at set time periods such as three or six months. At the end of each period, the bank adds the interest earned to the account. During the next period, the bank pays interest on all the money in the bank, including interest. In this way, the account earns interest on interest.

Suppose Ms. Tanner has $1000 in an account that is compounded quarterly at 5%. Find the balance after the first two quarters.

Use $I = prt$ to find the interest earned in the first quarter if $p = 1000$ and $r = 5\%$. Why is t equal to $\frac{1}{4}$?

First quarter: $I = 1000 \times 0.05 \times \frac{1}{4}$

$\qquad\qquad I = 12.50$

The interest, $12.50, earned in the first quarter is added to $1000. The principal becomes $1012.50.

Second quarter: $I = 1012.50 \times 0.05 \times \frac{1}{4}$

$\qquad\qquad I = 12.65625$ The interest in the second quarter is $12.66.

The balance after two quarters is $1012.50 + 12.66 or $1025.16.

Answer each of the following questions.

1. How much interest is earned in the third quarter of Ms. Tanner's account?

2. What is the balance in her account after three quarters?

3. What is the balance in her account after one year?

4. Suppose Ms. Tanner's account is compounded semiannually. What is the balance at the end of six months?

5. What is the balance after one year if her account is compounded semiannually?

Compound Interest

In most banks, interest on savings accounts is compounded at
set time periods such as three or six months. At the end of each
period, the bank adds the interest earned to the account.
During the next period, the bank pays interest on all the money
in the bank, including interest. In this way, the account earns
interest on interest.

Suppose Ms. Tanner has $1000 in an account that is compounded
quarterly at 5%. Find the balance after the first two quarters.

Use $I = prt$ to find the interest earned in the first quarter if
$p = 1000$ and $r = 5\%$. Why is t equal to $\frac{1}{4}$?

First quarter: $I = 1000 \times 0.05 \times \frac{1}{4}$

$I = 12.50$

The interest, $12.50, earned in the first quarter is added to
$1000. The principal becomes $1012.50.

Second quarter: $I = 1012.50 \times 0.05 \times \frac{1}{4}$

$I = 12.65625$ The interest in the second
quarter is $12.66.

The balance after two quarters is $1012.50 + 12.66 or $1025.16.

Answer each of the following questions.

1. How much interest is earned in the third quarter of
   Ms. Tanner's account? $I = \$12.81$

2. What is the balance in her account after three quarters?
   $1037.97

3. What is the balance in her account after one year?
   $1050.94

4. Suppose Ms. Tanner's account is compounded semiannually.
   What is the balance at the end of six months? **$1025.00**

5. What is the balance after one year if her account is
   compounded semiannually? **$1050.63**

5-6

Enrichment

Geometric Probability

If a dart, thrown at random, hits a triangular board shown at the right, what is the probability that it will hit the shaded region? This probability can be determined by comparing the area of the shaded region to the area of the board. This ratio indicates what fraction of the tosses should hit in the shaded region.

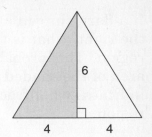

$$\frac{\text{area of shaded region}}{\text{area of triangular board}} = \frac{\frac{1}{2}(4)(6)}{\frac{1}{2}(8)(6)}$$

$$= \frac{12}{24} \text{ or } \frac{1}{2}$$

In general, if S is a subregion of some region R, then the probability, $P(S)$, that a point, chosen at random, belongs to subregion S is given by the following.

$$P(S) = \frac{\text{area of subregion } S}{\text{area of region } R}$$

Find the probability that a point, chosen at random, belongs to the shaded subregions of the following regions.

1.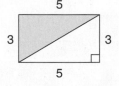

2.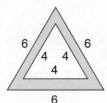

3.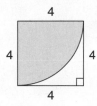

4.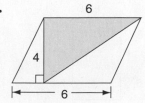

5.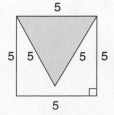

6.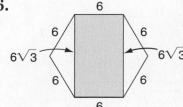

7.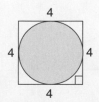

8.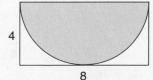

9.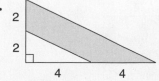

Geometric Probability

If a dart, thrown at random, hits a triangular board shown at
the right, what is the probability that it will hit the shaded
region? This probability can be determined by comparing the
area of the shaded region to the area of the board. This ratio
indicates what fraction of the tosses should hit in the shaded
region.

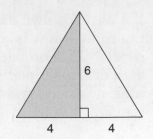

$$\frac{\text{area of shaded region}}{\text{area of triangular board}} = \frac{\frac{1}{2}(4)(6)}{\frac{1}{2}(8)(6)}$$

$$= \frac{12}{24} \text{ or } \frac{1}{2}$$

In general, if S is a subregion of some region R, then the
probability, $P(S)$, that a point, chosen at random, belongs to
subregion S is given by the following.

$$P(S) = \frac{\text{area of subregion } S}{\text{area of region } R}$$

**Find the probability that a point, chosen at random, belongs
to the shaded subregions of the following regions.**

1. 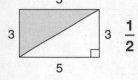 $\dfrac{1}{2}$

2. 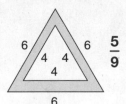 $\dfrac{5}{9}$

3. $\dfrac{\pi}{4}$

4. 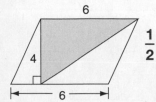 $\dfrac{1}{2}$

5. 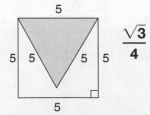 $\dfrac{\sqrt{3}}{4}$

6. 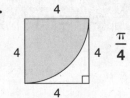 $\dfrac{2}{3}$

7. 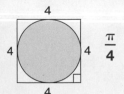 $\dfrac{\pi}{4}$

8. 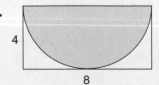 $\dfrac{\pi}{4}$

9. 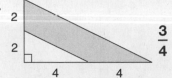 $\dfrac{3}{4}$

5-7

Enrichment

Conditional Probability

The probability of an event given the occurrence of another event is called **conditional probability.** The conditional probability of event A given event B is denoted $P(A|B)$.

Example: Suppose a pair of number cubes is rolled. It is known that the sum is greater than seven. Find the probability that the number cubes match.

There are 15 sums greater than seven and there are 36 possible pairs altogether.

$$P(B) = \frac{15}{36}$$

There are three matching pairs greater than seven, (4, 4), (5, 5), and (6, 6).

$$P(A \text{ and } B) = \frac{3}{36}$$

$$P(A|B) = \frac{P(A \text{ and } B)}{P(B)}$$

$$= \frac{\frac{3}{36}}{\frac{15}{36}} \text{ or } \frac{1}{5}$$

The conditional probability is $\frac{1}{5}$.

A card is drawn from a standard deck of 52 cards and is found to be red. Given that event, find each of the following probabilities.

1. P(heart)

2. P(ace)

3. P(face card)

4. P(jack or ten)

5. P(six of spades)

6. P(six of hearts)

A sports survey taken at Stirers High School shows that 48% of the respondents liked soccer, 66% liked basketball, and 38% liked hockey. Also, 30% liked soccer and basketball, 22% liked basketball and hockey and 28% liked soccer and hockey. Finally, 12% liked all three sports.

7. Find the probability that Meg likes soccer if she likes basketball.

8. Find the probability that Juan likes basketball if he likes soccer.

9. Find the probability that Mieko likes hockey if she likes basketball.

10. Find the probability that Greg likes hockey if he likes soccer.

Conditional Probability

The probability of an event given the occurrence of another event is called **conditional probability.** The conditional probability of event A given event B is denoted $P(A|B)$.

Example: Suppose a pair of number cubes is rolled. It is known that the sum is greater than seven. Find the probability that the number cubes match.

There are 15 sums greater than seven and there are 36 possible pairs altogether.

There are three matching pairs greater than seven, (4, 4), (5, 5), and (6, 6).

$$P(B) = \frac{15}{36}$$

$$P(A \text{ and } B) = \frac{3}{36}$$

$$P(A|B) = \frac{P(A \text{ and } B)}{P(B)}$$

$$= \frac{\frac{3}{36}}{\frac{15}{36}} \text{ or } \frac{1}{5}$$

The conditional probability is $\frac{1}{5}$.

A card is drawn from a standard deck of 52 cards and is found to be red. Given that event, find each of the following probabilities.

1. $P(\text{heart})$ $\frac{1}{2}$

2. $P(\text{ace})$ $\frac{1}{13}$

3. $P(\text{face card})$ $\frac{3}{13}$

4. $P(\text{jack or ten})$ $\frac{2}{13}$

5. $P(\text{six of spades})$ **0**

6. $P(\text{six of hearts})$ $\frac{1}{26}$

A sports survey taken at Stirers High School shows that 48% of the respondents liked soccer, 66% liked basketball, and 38% liked hockey. Also, 30% liked soccer and basketball, 22% liked basketball and hockey and 28% liked soccer and hockey. Finally, 12% liked all three sports.

7. Find the probability that Meg likes soccer if she likes basketball. $\frac{5}{11}$

8. Find the probability that Juan likes basketball if he likes soccer. $\frac{5}{8}$

9. Find the probability that Mieko likes hockey if she likes basketball. $\frac{1}{3}$

10. Find the probability that Greg likes hockey if he likes soccer. $\frac{7}{12}$

 Algebra: Concepts and Applications

NAME _____ DATE _____ PERIOD _____

Enrichment

Student Edition
Pages 238–243

The Tower of Hanoi

The Tower of Hanoi puzzle has three pegs, with a stack of disks on peg a. The object is to move all of the disks to another peg. You may move only one disk at a time. Also, a larger disk may never be put on top of a smaller disk.

A chart has been started to record your moves as you solve the puzzle.

Another way to record the moves is to use letters. For example, the first two steps in the chart can be recorded as 1c, 2b. This shows that disk 1 is moved to peg c, and then disk 2 is moved to peg b.

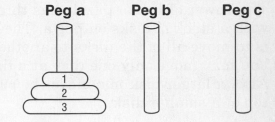

Peg a	Peg b	Peg c
1 2 3		
2 3		1
3	2	1

Solve each problem.

1. Finish the chart to solve the Tower of Hanoi puzzle for three disks.

2. Record your solution using letters.

3. On a separate sheet of paper, solve the puzzle for four disks. Record your solution.

4. Solve the puzzle for five disks. Record your solution.

5. If you start with an odd number of disks and you want to end with the stack on peg c, what should be your first move?

6. If you start with an even number of disks and you want to end with the stack on peg b, what should be your first move?

35

Algebra: Concepts and Applications

6–1

Enrichment

Student Edition
Pages 238–243

The Tower of Hanoi

The Tower of Hanoi puzzle has three pegs, with a stack of disks on peg a. The object is to move all of the disks to another peg. You may move only one disk at a time. Also, a larger disk may never be put on top of a smaller disk.

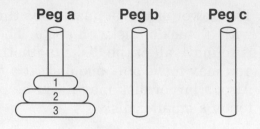

Peg a   Peg b   Peg c

A chart has been started to record your moves as you solve the puzzle.

Another way to record the moves is to use letters. For example, the first two steps in the chart can be recorded as 1c, 2b. This shows that disk 1 is moved to peg c, and then disk 2 is moved to peg b.

Solve each problem.

1. Finish the chart to solve the Tower of Hanoi puzzle for three disks.

2. Record your solution using letters.
   1c, 2b, 1b, 3c, 1a, 2c, 1c

3. On a separate sheet of paper, solve the puzzle for four disks. Record your solution.
   1c, 2b, 1b, 3c, 1a, 2c, 1c,
   4b, 1b, 2a, 1a, 3b, 1c, 2b, 1b

4. Solve the puzzle for five disks. Record your solution.
   1c, 2b, 1b, 3c, 1a, 2c, 1c, 4b, 1b, 2a, 1a, 3b,
   1c, 2b, 1b, 5c, 1a, 2c, 1c, 3a, 1b, 2a, 1a, 4c,
   1c, 2b, 1b, 3c, 1a, 2c, 1c

5. If you start with an odd number of disks and you want to end with the stack on peg c, what should be your first move?
   1c

6. If you start with an even number of disks and you want to end with the stack on peg b, what should be your first move?
   1c

Peg a	Peg b	Peg c
1 2 3		
2 3		1
3	2	1
3	1 2	
	1 2	3
1	2	3
1		2 3
		1 2 3

Enrichment

Diophantine Equations

The first great algebraist, Diophantus of Alexandria (about
A.D. 300), devoted much of his work to the solving of
indeterminate equations. An indeterminate equation has
more than one variable and an unlimited number of solutions.
An example is $x + 2y = 4$.

When the coefficients of an indeterminate equation are integers
and you are asked to find solutions that must be integers, the
equation is called a **diophantine equation**. Such equations
can be quite difficult to solve, often involving trial and error—
and some luck!

*Solve each diophantine equation by finding at least one pair
of positive integers that makes the equation true. Some hints
are given to help you.*

1. $2x + 5y = 32$

    a. First solve the equation for x.

    b. Why must y be an even number?

    c. Find at least one solution.

2. $5x + 2y = 42$

    a. First solve the equation for x.

    b. Rewrite your answer in the form $x = 8 +$ some expression.

    c. Why must $(2 - 2y)$ be a multiple of 5?

    d. Find at least one solution.

3. $2x + 7y = 29$ **4.** $7x + 5y = 118$

5. $8x - 13y = 100$ **6.** $3x + 4y = 22$

7. $5x - 14y = 11$ **8.** $7x + 3y = 40$

6-2 Enrichment

Diophantine Equations

The first great algebraist, Diophantus of Alexandria (about A.D. 300), devoted much of his work to the solving of indeterminate equations. An indeterminate equation has more than one variable and an unlimited number of solutions. An example is $x + 2y = 4$.

When the coefficients of an indeterminate equation are integers and you are asked to find solutions that must be integers, the equation is called a **diophantine equation**. Such equations can be quite difficult to solve, often involving trial and error—and some luck!

Solve each diophantine equation by finding at least one pair of positive integers that makes the equation true. Some hints are given to help you.

1. $2x + 5y = 32$

   a. First solve the equation for x. $x = 16 - \dfrac{5y}{2}$

   b. Why must y be an even number? **If y is odd, then x won't be an integer.**

   c. Find at least one solution. **any of these: (11, 2), (6, 4), (1, 6)**

2. $5x + 2y = 42$

   a. First solve the equation for x. $x = \dfrac{42 - 2y}{5}$

   b. Rewrite your answer in the form $x = 8 +$ some expression. $x = 8 + \dfrac{2 - 2y}{5}$

   c. Why must $(2 - 2y)$ be a multiple of 5? **otherwise, x won't be an integer**

   d. Find at least one solution. **any of these: (8, 1), (6, 6), (4, 11), (2, 16)**

3. $2x + 7y = 29$
   (11, 1) or (4, 3)

4. $7x + 5y = 118$
   any of these: (14, 4), (9, 11), (4, 18)

5. $8x - 13y = 100$
   (19, 4), (32, 12) or any pair when $y = 4n$ and n is a positive odd number

6. $3x + 4y = 22$
   (6, 1) or (2, 4)

7. $5x - 14y = 11$
   (5, 1), (19, 6) or any pair when $y = 5m - 4$ and m is a positive number

8. $7x + 3y = 40$
   (4, 4) or (1, 11)

 Algebra: Concepts and Applications

6-3

Enrichment

Student Edition
Pages 250–255

Taxicab Graphs

You have used a rectangular coordinate system to graph equations such as $y = x - 1$ on a coordinate plane. In a coordinate plane, the numbers in an ordered pair (x, y) can be any two real numbers.

**Taxicab Graph
of $y = x - 1$**

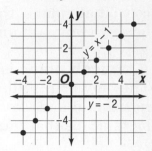

A **taxicab plane** is different from the usual coordinate plane. The only points allowed are those that exist along the horizontal and vertical grid lines. You may think of the points as taxicabs that must stay on the streets.

The taxicab graph shows the equations $y = -2$ and $y = x - 1$. Notice that one of the graphs is no longer a straight line. It is now a collection of separate points.

Graph these equations on the taxicab plane at the right.

1. $y = x + 1$

2. $y = -2x + 3$

3. $y = 2.5$

4. $x = -4$

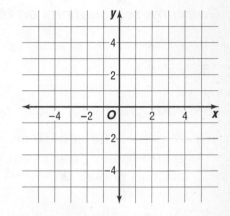

Use your graphs for these problems.

5. Which of the equations would have the same graph in both the usual coordinate plane and the taxicab plane?

6. Describe the form of equations that have the same graph in both the usual coordinate plane and the taxicab plane.

In the taxicab plane, distances are not measured diagonally, but along the streets. Write the taxi-distance between each pair of points.

7. (0, 0) and (5, 2)

8. (0, 0) and (−3, 2)

9. (0, 0) and (2, 1.5)

10. (1, 2) and (4, 3)

11. (2, 4) and (−1, 3)

12. (0, 4) and (−2, 0)

Draw these graphs on the taxicab grid at the right.

13. The set of points whose taxi-distance from (0, 0) is 2 units.

14. The set of points whose taxi-distance from (2, 1) is 3 units.

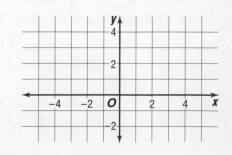

6-3

Enrichment

Student Edition
Pages 250–255

Taxicab Graphs

You have used a rectangular coordinate system to graph equations such as $y = x - 1$ on a coordinate plane. In a coordinate plane, the numbers in an ordered pair (x, y) can be any two real numbers.

Taxicab Graph of $y = x - 1$

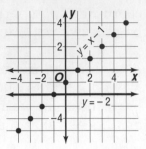

A **taxicab plane** is different from the usual coordinate plane. The only points allowed are those that exist along the horizontal and vertical grid lines. You may think of the points as taxicabs that must stay on the streets.

The taxicab graph shows the equations $y = -2$ and $y = x - 1$. Notice that one of the graphs is no longer a straight line. It is now a collection of separate points.

Graph these equations on the taxicab plane at the right.

1. $y = x + 1$
2. $y = -2x + 3$
3. $y = 2.5$
4. $x = -4$

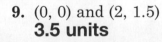

Use your graphs for these problems.

5. Which of the equations would have the same graph in both the usual coordinate plane and the taxicab plane? **$x = -4$**

6. Describe the form of equations that have the same graph in both the usual coordinate plane and the taxicab plane.
   $x = A$ and $y = B$, where A and B are integers

In the taxicab plane, distances are not measured diagonally, but along the streets. Write the taxi-distance between each pair of points.

7. $(0, 0)$ and $(5, 2)$
   7 units
8. $(0, 0)$ and $(-3, 2)$
   5 units
9. $(0, 0)$ and $(2, 1.5)$
   3.5 units

10. $(1, 2)$ and $(4, 3)$
    4 units
11. $(2, 4)$ and $(-1, 3)$
    4 units
12. $(0, 4)$ and $(-2, 0)$
    6 units

Draw these graphs on the taxicab grid at the right.

13. The set of points whose taxi-distance from $(0, 0)$ is 2 units. **indicated by crosses**

14. The set of points whose taxi-distance from $(2, 1)$ is 3 units. **indicated by dots**

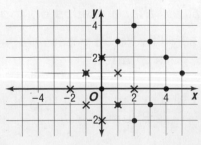

Composite Functions

Three things are needed to have a function—a set called the *domain,* a set called the *range,* and a *rule* that matches each element in the domain with only one element in the range. Here is an example.

Rule: $f(x) = 2x + 1$

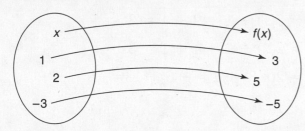

$f(x) = 2x + 1$

$f(1) = 2(1) + 1 = 2 + 1 = 3$

$f(2) = 2(2) + 1 = 4 + 1 = 5$

$f(-3) = 2(-3) + 1 = -6 + 1 = -5$

Suppose we have three sets A, B, and C and two functions described as shown below.

Rule: $f(x) = 2x + 1$ Rule: $g(y) = 3y - 4$

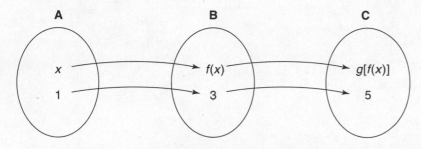

$g(y) = 3y - 4$
$g(3) = 3(3) - 4 = 5$

Let's find a rule that will match elements of set A with elements of set C without finding any elements in set B. In other words, let's find a rule for the **composite function** $g[f(x)]$.

Since $f(x) = 2x + 1$, $g[f(x)] = g(2x + 1)$.
Since $g(y) = 3y - 4$, $g(2x + 1) = 3(2x + 1) - 4$, or $6x - 1$.
Therefore, $g[f(x)] = 6x - 1$.

Find a rule for the composite function g[f(x)].

1. $f(x) = 3x$ and $g(y) = 2y + 1$

2. $f(x) = x^2 + 1$ and $g(y) = 4y$

3. $f(x) = -2x$ and $g(y) = y^2 - 3y$

4. $f(x) = \dfrac{1}{x - 3}$ and $g(y) = y^{-1}$

5. Is it always the case that $g[f(x)] = f[g(x)]$? Justify your answer.

Composite Functions

Three things are needed to have a function—a set called the
domain, a set called the *range,* and a *rule* that matches each
element in the domain with only one element in the range.
Here is an example.

Rule: $f(x) = 2x + 1$

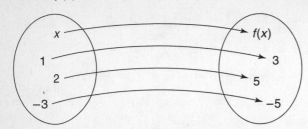

$f(x) = 2x + 1$

$f(1) = 2(1) + 1 = 2 + 1 = 3$

$f(2) = 2(2) + 1 = 4 + 1 = 5$

$f(-3) = 2(-3) + 1 = -6 + 1 = -5$

Suppose we have three sets A, B, and C and two functions
described as shown below.

Rule: $f(x) = 2x + 1$ Rule: $g(y) = 3y - 4$

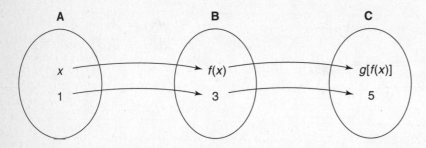

$g(y) = 3y - 4$
$g(3) = 3(3) - 4 = 5$

Let's find a rule that will match elements of set A with
elements of set C without finding any elements in set B. In
other words, let's find a rule for the **composite function**
$g[f(x)]$.

Since $f(x) = 2x + 1$, $g[f(x)] = g(2x + 1)$.
Since $g(y) = 3y - 4$, $g(2x + 1) = 3(2x + 1) - 4$, or $6x - 1$.
Therefore, $g[f(x)] = 6x - 1$.

Find a rule for the composite function g[f(x)].

1. $f(x) = 3x$ and $g(y) = 2y + 1$
   $g[f(x)] = 6x + 1$

2. $f(x) = x^2 + 1$ and $g(y) = 4y$
   $g[f(x)] = 4x^2 + 4$

3. $f(x) = -2x$ and $g(y) = y^2 - 3y$
   $g[f(x)] = 4x^2 + 6x$

4. $f(x) = \dfrac{1}{x - 3}$ and $g(y) = y^{-1}$
   $g[f(x)] = x - 3$

5. Is it always the case that $g[f(x)] = f[g(x)]$? Justify your answer.
   **No. For example, in Exercise 1, $f[g(x)] = f(2x + 1) =$
   $3(2x + 1) = 6x + 3$, not $6x + 1$.**

Algebra: Concepts and Applications

6-5 Enrichment

nth Power Variation

An equation of the form $y = kx^n$, where $k \neq 0$, describes an nth power variation. The variable n can be replaced by 2 to indicate the second power of x (the square of x) or by 3 to indicate the third power of x (the cube of x).

Assume that the weight of a person of average build varies directly as the cube of that person's height. The equation of variation has the form $w = kh^3$.

The weight that a person's legs will support is proportional to the cross-sectional area of the leg bones. This area varies directly as the square of the person's height. The equation of variation has the form $s = kh^2$.

Answer each question.

1. For a person 6 feet tall who weighs 200 pounds, find a value for k in the equation $w = kh^3$.

2. Use your answer from Exercise 1 to predict the weight of a person who is 5 feet tall.

3. Find the value for k in the equation $w = kh^3$ for a baby who is 20 inches long and weighs 6 pounds.

4. How does your answer to Exercise 3 demonstrate that a baby is significantly fatter in proportion to its height than an adult?

5. For a person 6 feet tall who weighs 200 pounds, find a value for k in the equation $s = kh^2$.

6. For a baby who is 20 inches long and weighs 6 pounds, find an "infant value" for k in the equation $s = kh^2$.

7. According to the adult equation you found (Exercise 1), how much would an imaginary giant 20 feet tall weigh?

8. According to the adult equation for weight supported (Exercise 5), how much weight could a 20-foot tall giant's legs actually support?

9. What can you conclude from Exercises 7 and 8?

Algebra: Concepts and Applications

nth Power Variation

An equation of the form $y = kx^n$, where $k \neq 0$, describes an nth power variation. The variable n can be replaced by 2 to indicate the second power of x (the square of x) or by 3 to indicate the third power of x (the cube of x).

Assume that the weight of a person of average build varies directly as the cube of that person's height. The equation of variation has the form $w = kh^3$.

The weight that a person's legs will support is proportional to the cross-sectional area of the leg bones. This area varies directly as the square of the person's height. The equation of variation has the form $s = kh^2$.

Answer each question.

1. For a person 6 feet tall who weighs 200 pounds, find a value for k in the equation $w = kh^3$. **$k = 0.93$**

2. Use your answer from Exercise 1 to predict the weight of a person who is 5 feet tall. **about 116 pounds**

3. Find the value for k in the equation $w = kh^3$ for a baby who is 20 inches long and weighs 6 pounds.
   $k = 1.296$ for $h = \frac{5}{3}$ ft

4. How does your answer to Exercise 3 demonstrate that a baby is significantly fatter in proportion to its height than an adult? **k has a greater value.**

5. For a person 6 feet tall who weighs 200 pounds, find a value for k in the equation $s = kh^2$. **$k = 5.55$**

6. For a baby who is 20 inches long and weighs 6 pounds, find an "infant value" for k in the equation $s = kh^2$.
   $k = 2.16$ for $h = \frac{5}{3}$ ft

7. According to the adult equation you found (Exercise 1), how much would an imaginary giant 20 feet tall weigh?
   7440 pounds

8. According to the adult equation for weight supported (Exercise 5), how much weight could a 20-foot tall giant's legs actually support?
   only 2222 pounds

9. What can you conclude from Exercises 7 and 8?
   Sample answer: Bone strength limits the size humans can attain.

6-6

Enrichment

Student Edition
Pages 270–275

Analyzing Data

Fill in each table below. Then write inversely, or directly **to complete each conclusion.**

1.

l	2	4	8	16	32
w	4	4	4	4	4
A					

For a set of rectangles with a width of 4, the area varies _____ as the length.

2.

Hours	2	4	5	6
Speed	55	55	55	55
Distance				

For a car traveling at 55 mi/h, the distance covered varies _____ as the hours driven.

3.

Oat bran	$\frac{1}{3}$ cup	$\frac{2}{3}$ cup	1 cup
Water	1 cup	2 cup	3 cup
Servings	1	2	

The number of servings of oat bran varies _____ as the number of cups of oat bran.

4.

Hours of Work	128	128	128
People Working	2	4	8
Hours per Person			

A job requires 128 hours of work. The number of hours each person works varies _____ as the number of people working.

5.

Miles	100	100	100	100
Rate	20	25	50	100
Hours	5			

For a 100-mile car trip, the time the trip takes varies _____ as the average rate of speed the car travels.

6.

b	3	4	5	6
h	10	10	10	10
A	15			

For a set of right triangles with a height of 10, the area varies _____ as the base.

Use the table at the right.

7. x varies _____ as y.

8. z varies _____ as y.

9. x varies _____ as z.

x	1	1.5	2	2.5	3
y	2	3	4	5	6
z	60	40	30	24	20

Algebra: Concepts and Applications

NAME _____ DATE _____ PERIOD _____

Enrichment

Analyzing Data

Fill in each table below. Then write inversely, or directly **to complete each conclusion.**

1.

I	2	4	8	16	32
w	4	4	4	4	4
A	8	16	32	64	128

For a set of rectangles with a width of 4, the area varies **directly** as the length.

2.

Hours	2	4	5	6
Speed	55	55	55	55
Distance	165	220	275	330

For a car traveling at 55 mi/h, the distance covered varies **directly** as the hours driven.

3.

Oat bran	$\frac{1}{3}$ cup	$\frac{2}{3}$ cup	1 cup
Water	1 cup	2 cup	3 cup
Servings	1	2	3

The number of servings of oat bran varies **directly** as the number of cups of oat bran.

4.

Hours of Work	128	128	128
People Working	2	4	8
Hours per Person	64	32	16

A job requires 128 hours of work. The number of hours each person works varies **inversely** as the number of people working.

5.

Miles	100	100	100	100
Rate	20	25	50	100
Hours	5	4	2	1

For a 100-mile car trip, the time the trip takes varies **inversely** as the average rate of speed the car travels.

6.

b	3	4	5	6
h	10	10	10	10
A	15	20	25	30

For a set of right triangles with a height of 10, the area varies **directly** as the base.

Use the table at the right.

7. x varies **directly** as y.

8. z varies **inversely** as y.

9. x varies **inversely** as z.

x	1	1.5	2	2.5	3
y	2	3	4	5	6
z	60	40	30	24	20

Algebra: Concepts and Applications

Enrichment

Student Edition
Pages 284–289

Treasure Hunt with Slopes

Using the definition of slope, draw lines with the slopes listed below. A correct solution will trace the route to the treasure.

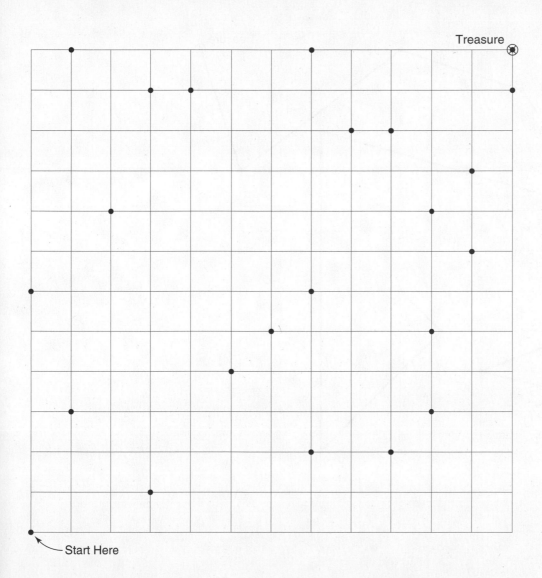

Treasure

Start Here

1. 3   **2.** $\dfrac{1}{4}$ **3.** $-\dfrac{2}{5}$ **4.** 0   **5.** 1   **6.** -1

7. no slope   **8.** $\dfrac{2}{7}$ **9.** $\dfrac{3}{2}$ **10.** $\dfrac{1}{3}$ **11.** $-\dfrac{3}{4}$ **12.** 3

Algebra: Concepts and Applications

Enrichment

Treasure Hunt with Slopes

Using the definition of slope, draw lines with the slopes listed below. A correct solution will trace the route to the treasure.

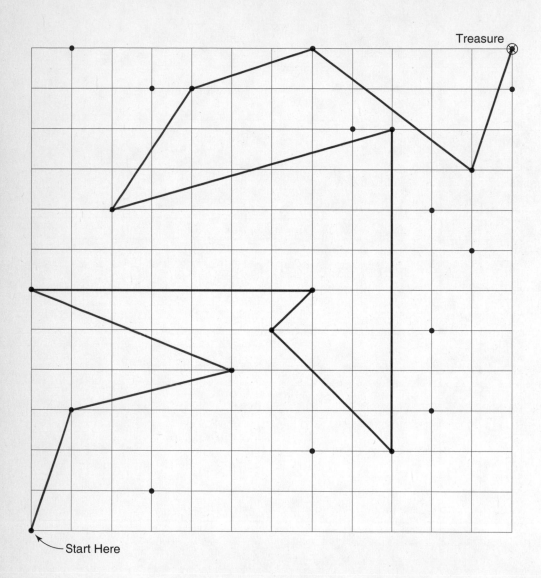

1. 3

2. $\dfrac{1}{4}$

3. $-\dfrac{2}{5}$

4. 0

5. 1

6. -1

7. no slope

8. $\dfrac{2}{7}$

9. $\dfrac{3}{2}$

10. $\dfrac{1}{3}$

11. $-\dfrac{3}{4}$

12. 3

Algebra: Concepts and Applications

Celsius and Kelvin Temperatures

If you blow up a balloon and put it in the refrigerator, the
balloon will shrink as the temperature of the air in the balloon
decreases.

The volume of a certain gas is measured at 30° Celsius. The
temperature is decreased and the volume is measured again.

Temperature (t)	Volume (v)
30°C	202 mL
21°C	196 mL
0°C	182 mL
−12°C	174 mL
−27°C	164 mL

1. Graph this table on the coordinate plane provided below.

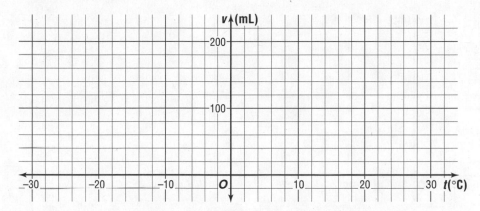

2. Find the equation of the line that passes through the points
   you graphed in Exercise 1.

3. Use the equation you found in Exercise 2 to find the
   temperature that would give a volume of zero. This
   temperature is the lowest one possible and is called
   "absolute zero."

4. In 1848 Lord Kelvin proposed a new temperature scale with
   0 being assigned to absolute zero. The size of the degree
   chosen was the same size as the Celsius degree. Change each
   of the Celsius temperatures in the table above to degrees
   Kelvin.

7-2

Enrichment

Celsius and Kelvin Temperatures

If you blow up a balloon and put it in the refrigerator, the balloon will shrink as the temperature of the air in the balloon decreases.

The volume of a certain gas is measured at 30° Celsius. The temperature is decreased and the volume is measured again.

Temperature (t)	Volume (v)
30°C	202 mL
21°C	196 mL
0°C	182 mL
−12°C	174 mL
−27°C	164 mL

1. Graph this table on the coordinate plane provided below.

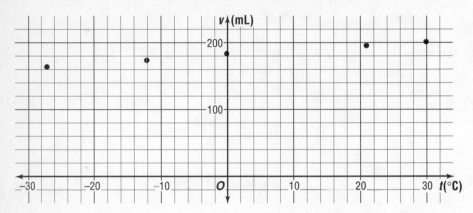

2. Find the equation of the line that passes through the points you graphed in Exercise 1. $y = \frac{2}{3}x + 182$ or $v = \frac{2}{3}t + 182$

3. Use the equation you found in Exercise 2 to find the temperature that would give a volume of zero. This temperature is the lowest one possible and is called "absolute zero." **−273°C**

4. In 1848 Lord Kelvin proposed a new temperature scale with 0 being assigned to absolute zero. The size of the degree chosen was the same size as the Celsius degree. Change each of the Celsius temperatures in the table above to degrees Kelvin. **303°, 294°, 273°, 261°, 246°**

Algebra: Concepts and Applications

Ideal Weight

You can find your ideal weight as follows.
A woman should weigh 100 pounds for the first 5 feet of height and 5 additional pounds for each inch over 5 feet (5 feet = 60 inches). A man should weigh 106 pounds for the first 5 feet of height and 6 additional pounds for each inch over 5 feet. These formulas apply to people with normal bone structures.

To determine your bone structure, wrap your thumb and index finger around the wrist of your other hand. If the thumb and finger just touch, you have normal bone structure. If they overlap, you are small-boned. If they don't overlap, you are large-boned. Small-boned people should decrease their calculated ideal weight by 10%. Large-boned people should increase the value by 10%.

Calculate the ideal weights of these people.

1. woman, 5 ft 4 in., normal-boned

2. man, 5 ft 11 in., large-boned

3. man, 6 ft 5 in., small-boned

4. you, if you are at least 5 ft tall

Suppose a normal-boned man is x inches tall. If he is at least 5 feet tall, then x − 60 represents the number of inches this man is over 5 feet tall. For each of these inches, his ideal weight is increased by 6 pounds. Thus, his proper weight (y) is given by the formula y = 6(x − 60) + 106 or y = 6x − 254. If the man is large-boned, the formula becomes y = 6x − 254 + 0.10(6x − 254).

5. Write the formula for the weight of a large-boned man in slope-intercept form.

6. Derive the formula for the ideal weight (y) of a normal-boned female with height x inches. Write the formula in slope-intercept form.

7. Derive the formula in slope-intercept form for the ideal weight (y) of a large-boned female with height x inches.

8. Derive the formula in slope-intercept form for the ideal weight (y) of a small-boned male with height x inches.

9. Find the heights at which normal-boned males and large-boned females would weigh the same.

Enrichment

Ideal Weight

You can find your ideal weight as follows.
A woman should weigh 100 pounds for the first 5 feet of height
and 5 additional pounds for each inch over 5 feet (5 feet =
60 inches). A man should weigh 106 pounds for the first 5 feet
of height and 6 additional pounds for each inch over 5 feet.
These formulas apply to people with normal bone structures.

To determine your bone structure, wrap your thumb and index
finger around the wrist of your other hand. If the thumb and
finger just touch, you have normal bone structure. If they
overlap, you are small-boned. If they don't overlap, you are
large-boned. Small-boned people should decrease their
calculated ideal weight by 10%. Large-boned people should
increase the value by 10%.

Calculate the ideal weights of these people.

1. woman, 5 ft 4 in., normal-boned
   120 lb

2. man, 5 ft 11 in., large-boned
   189.2 lb

3. man, 6 ft 5 in., small-boned
   187.2 lb

4. you, if you are at least 5 ft tall
   See students' work.

*Suppose a normal-boned man is x inches tall. If he is at
least 5 feet tall, then x − 60 represents the number of inches
this man is over 5 feet tall. For each of these inches, his
ideal weight is increased by 6 pounds. Thus, his proper
weight (y) is given by the formula $y = 6(x − 60) + 106$ or
$y = 6x − 254$. If the man is large-boned, the formula becomes
$y = 6x − 254 + 0.10(6x − 254)$.*

5. Write the formula for the weight of a large-boned man in
   slope-intercept form.
   $y = 6.6x − 279.4$

6. Derive the formula for the ideal weight (y) of a normal-
   boned female with height x inches. Write the formula in
   slope-intercept form.
   $y = 5x − 200$

7. Derive the formula in slope-intercept form for the ideal
   weight (y) of a large-boned female with height x inches.
   $y = 5.5x − 220$

8. Derive the formula in slope-intercept form for the ideal
   weight (y) of a small-boned male with height x inches.
   $y = 5.4x − 228.6$

9. Find the heights at which normal-boned males and large-
   boned females would weigh the same.
   68 in., or 5 ft 8 in.

7-4 **Enrichment**

Student Edition
Pages 302–307

A Scatter Plot

Each point on the graph shows the relation between the number of people attending the Roxy Cinema and the number of cars in the parking lot.

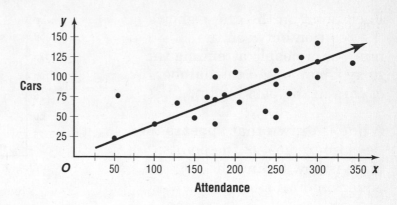

A line is drawn that appears to lie close to most of the points. Here is how to find the equation of this line.

The line passes through (100, 40) and (300, 120). Use the slope-intercept form.

$$m = \frac{120 - 40}{300 - 100}$$

$$= \frac{80}{200}$$

$$= \frac{2}{5}$$

$$y = mx + b$$

$$40 = \frac{2}{5}(100) + b$$

$$0 = b$$

An equation for the line is $y = \frac{2}{5}x$.

Solve each problem.

1. Suppose the owner of the Roxy decides to increase the seating capacity of the theater to 1000. How many cars should the parking lot be prepared to accommodate?

2. The points (240, 60) and (340, 120) lie on the scatter plot. Write an equation for the line through these points.

3. Do you think the equation in Exercise 2 is a good representation of the relationship in this problem?

4. Suppose the equation for the relationship between attendance at the theater and cars in the parking lot is $y = 2x + 20$. What might you suspect about the users of the parking lot?

Algebra: Concepts and Applications

A Scatter Plot

Each point on the graph shows the relation between the number of people attending the Roxy Cinema and the number of cars in the parking lot.

A line is drawn that appears to lie close to most of the points. Here is how to find the equation of this line.

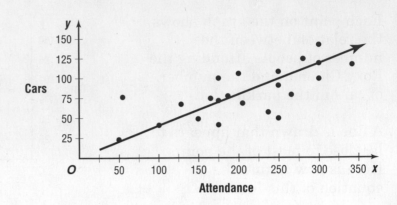

The line passes through (100, 40) and (300, 120). Use the slope-intercept form.

$$m = \frac{120 - 40}{300 - 100}$$

$$= \frac{80}{200}$$

$$= \frac{2}{5}$$

$$y = mx + b$$

$$40 = \frac{2}{5}(100) + b$$

$$0 = b$$

An equation for the line is $y = \frac{2}{5}x$.

Solve each problem.

1. Suppose the owner of the Roxy decides to increase the seating capacity of the theater to 1000. How many cars should the parking lot be prepared to accommodate? **400 cars**

2. The points (240, 60) and (340, 120) lie on the scatter plot. Write an equation for the line through these points. $y = \frac{3}{5}x - 84$

3. Do you think the equation in Exercise 2 is a good representation of the relationship in this problem?
   No. The graph of the equation does not appear to go through the center of the data points.

4. Suppose the equation for the relationship between attendance at the theater and cars in the parking lot is $y = 2x + 20$. What might you suspect about the users of the parking lot?
   Many people are parking in the lot who are not going to the Roxy.

Equations of Lines and Planes in Intercept Form

One form that a linear equation may take is **intercept form.** The constants a and b are the x- and y-intercepts of the graph.

$$\frac{x}{a} + \frac{y}{b} = 1$$

In three-dimensional space, the equation of a plane takes a similar form.

$$\frac{x}{a} + \frac{y}{b} + \frac{z}{c} = 1$$

Here, the constants a, b, and c are the points where the plane meets the x, y, and z-axes.

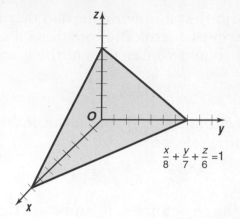

$$\frac{x}{8} + \frac{y}{7} + \frac{z}{6} = 1$$

Solve each problem.

1. Graph the equation $\dfrac{x}{3} + \dfrac{y}{2} + \dfrac{z}{1} = 1$.

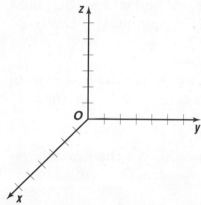

2. For the plane in Exercise 1, write an equation for the line where the plane intersects the xy-plane. Use intercept forms.

3. Write an equation for the line where the plane intersects the xz-plane.

4. Write an equation for the line where the plane intersects the yz-plane.

5. Graph the equation $\dfrac{x}{1} + \dfrac{y}{4} + \dfrac{z}{2} = 1$.

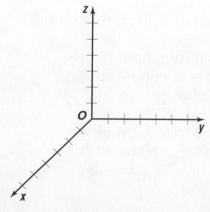

6. Write an equation for the xy-plane.

7. Write an equation for the yz-plane.

8. Write an equation for a plane parallel to the xy-plane with a z-intercept of 2.

9. Write an equation for a plane parallel to the yz-plane with an x-intercept of -3.

NAME _____ DATE _____ PERIOD _____

Enrichment

Equations of Lines and Planes in Intercept Form

One form that a linear equation may take is **intercept form**. The constants a and b are the x- and y-intercepts of the graph.

$$\frac{x}{a} + \frac{y}{b} = 1$$

In three-dimensional space, the equation of a plane takes a similar form.

$$\frac{x}{a} + \frac{y}{b} + \frac{z}{c} = 1$$

Here, the constants a, b, and c are the points where the plane meets the x, y, and z-axes.

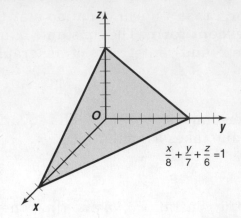

$$\frac{x}{8} + \frac{y}{7} + \frac{z}{6} = 1$$

Solve each problem.

1. Graph the equation $\frac{x}{3} + \frac{y}{2} + \frac{z}{1} = 1$.

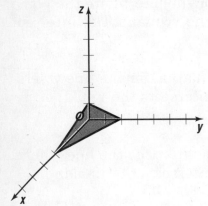

2. For the plane in Exercise 1, write an equation for the line where the plane intersects the xy-plane. Use intercept forms. $\frac{x}{3} + \frac{y}{2} = 1$

3. Write an equation for the line where the plane intersects the xz-plane.
$\frac{x}{3} + \frac{z}{1} = 1$

4. Write an equation for the line where the plane intersects the yz-plane.
$\frac{y}{2} + \frac{z}{1} = 1$

5. Graph the equation $\frac{x}{1} + \frac{y}{4} + \frac{z}{2} = 1$.

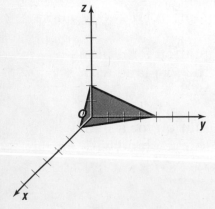

6. Write an equation for the xy-plane.
$z = 0$

7. Write an equation for the yz-plane.
$x = 0$

8. Write an equation for a plane parallel to the xy-plane with a z-intercept of 2. $z = 2$

9. Write an equation for a plane parallel to the yz-plane with an x-intercept of -3. $x = -3$

Algebra: Concepts and Applications

7-6

Enrichment

Inverse Relations

On each grid below, plot the points in Sets A and B. Then connect the points in Set A with the corresponding points in Set B. Then find the inverses of Set A and Set B, plot the two sets, and connect those points.

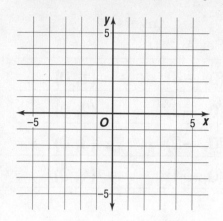

Set A	Set B
(−4, 0)	(0, 1)
(−3, 0)	(0, 2)
(−2, 0)	(0, 3)
(−1, 0)	(0, 4)

Inverse

	Set A	Set B
1.		
2.		
3.		
4.		

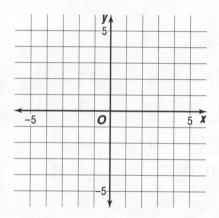

Set A	Set B
(−3, −3)	(−2, 1)
(−2, −2)	(−1, 2)
(−1, −1)	(0, 3)
(0, 0)	(1, 4)

Inverse

	Set A	Set B
5.		
6.		
7.		
8.		

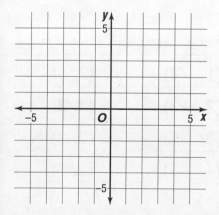

Set A	Set B
(−4, 1)	(3, 2)
(−3, 2)	(3, 2)
(−2, 3)	(3, 2)
(−1, 4)	(3, 2)

Inverse

	Set A	Set B
9.		
10.		
11.		
12.		

13. What is the graphical relationship between the line segments you drew connecting points in Sets A and B and the line segments connecting points in the inverses of those two sets?

Inverse Relations

On each grid below, plot the points in Sets A and B. Then connect the points in Set A with the corresponding points in Set B. Then find the inverses of Set A and Set B, plot the two sets, and connect those points.

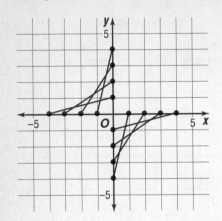

Set A	Set B
(−4, 0)	(0, 1)
(−3, 0)	(0, 2)
(−2, 0)	(0, 3)
(−1, 0)	(0, 4)

Inverse

	Set A	Set B
1.	**(0, −4)**	**(1, 0)**
2.	**(0, −3)**	**(2, 0)**
3.	**(0, −2)**	**(3, 0)**
4.	**(0, −1)**	**(4, 0)**

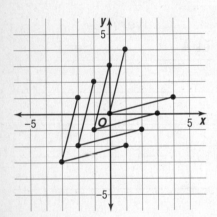

Set A	Set B
(−3, −3)	(−2, 1)
(−2, −2)	(−1, 2)
(−1, −1)	(0, 3)
(0, 0)	(1, 4)

Inverse

	Set A	Set B
5.	**(−3, −3)**	**(1, −2)**
6.	**(−2, −2)**	**(2, −1)**
7.	**(−1, −1)**	**(3, 0)**
8.	**(0, 0)**	**(4, 1)**

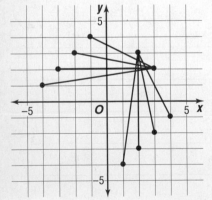

Set A	Set B
(−4, 1)	(3, 2)
(−3, 2)	(3, 2)
(−2, 3)	(3, 2)
(−1, 4)	(3, 2)

Inverse

	Set A	Set B
9.	**(1, −4)**	**(2, 3)**
10.	**(2, −3)**	**(2, 3)**
11.	**(3, −2)**	**(2, 3)**
12.	**(4, −1)**	**(2, 3)**

13. What is the graphical relationship between the line segments you drew connecting points in Sets A and B and the line segments connecting points in the inverses of those two sets? **Sample answer: The graphs are reflected across the line x = y by their inverses.**

Algebra: Concepts and Applications

Using Coordinates

1. Graph the points (1, 1), (4, 4), and (2, 4) on the coordinate system below. Connect the dots. Name the figure formed.

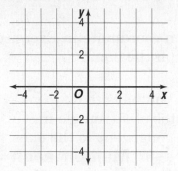

2. Multiply each *y*-coordinate by ⁻1. Graph the points. How is this triangle related to the one in Exercise 1?

3. Multiply each coordinate in Exercise 1 by ⁻1. Graph the points.

4. What would you have to do to get the coordinates of a triangle in Quadrant II congruent to the ones in Exercises 1–3?

5. Graph the points (3, 1), (2, 3), (4, 6), and (5, 4) on the coordinate plane at the right. Connect the dots. The figure formed is called a parallelogram.

6. Add 2 to both coordinates of each point and graph the new coordinates. Name the figure formed.

7. Add ⁻4 to the *x*-coordinate of each point in Exercise 5 and graph the new coordinates. Is this figure also a parallelogram?

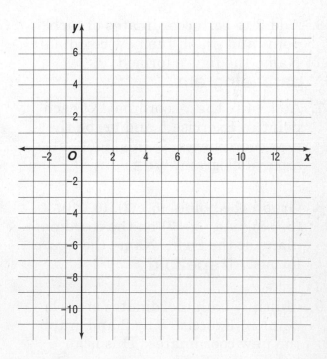

8. Graph the points (5, ⁻2), (6, ⁻3), (5, ⁻5), and (3, ⁻3) on the coordinate plane at the right. Name the figure formed.

9. Multiply both coordinates of each point in Exercise 8 by 2 and graph the new coordinates. This is an enlargement.

10. Multiply both coordinates of each point in Exercise 8 by $\frac{1}{2}$ and graph the new coordinates. This is a reduction.

Using Coordinates

1. Graph the points (1, 1), (4, 4), and (2, 4) on the coordinate system below. Connect the dots. Name the figure formed. **triangle**

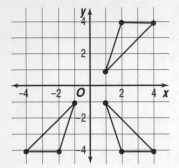

2. Multiply each *y*-coordinate by -1. Graph the points. How is this triangle related to the one in Exercise 1? **It is a reflection over the *x*-axis.**

3. Multiply each coordinate in Exercise 1 by -1. Graph the points.

4. What would you have to do to get the coordinates of a triangle in Quadrant II congruent to the ones in Exercises 1–3? **Multiply each *x*-coordinate in Exercise 1 by -1.**

5. Graph the points (3, 1), (2, 3), (4, 6), and (5, 4) on the coordinate plane at the right. Connect the dots. The figure formed is called a parallelogram.

6. Add 2 to both coordinates of each point and graph the new coordinates. Name the figure formed. **parallelogram**

7. Add -4 to the *x*-coordinate of each point in Exercise 5 and graph the new coordinates. Is this figure also a parallelogram? **yes**

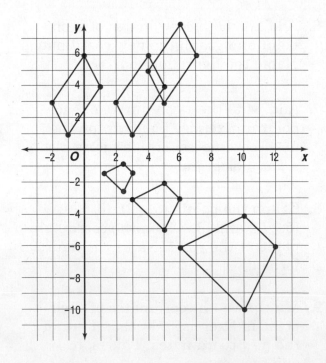

8. Graph the points (5, -2), (6, -3), (5, -5), and (3, -3) on the coordinate plane at the right. Name the figure formed. **trapezoid**

9. Multiply both coordinates of each point in Exercise 8 by 2 and graph the new coordinates. This is an enlargement.

10. Multiply both coordinates of each point in Exercise 8 by $\frac{1}{2}$ and graph the new coordinates. This is a reduction.

8-1

Enrichment

Patterns with Powers

Use your calculator, if necessary, to complete each pattern.

a. $2^{10} =$ _____

$2^9 =$ _____

$2^8 =$ _____

$2^7 =$ _____

$2^6 =$ _____

$2^5 =$ _____

$2^4 =$ _____

$2^3 =$ _____

$2^2 =$ _____

$2^1 =$ _____

b. $5^{10} =$ _____

$5^9 =$ _____

$5^8 =$ _____

$5^7 =$ _____

$5^6 =$ _____

$5^5 =$ _____

$5^4 =$ _____

$5^3 =$ _____

$5^2 =$ _____

$5^1 =$ _____

c. $4^{10} =$ _____

$4^9 =$ _____

$4^8 =$ _____

$4^7 =$ _____

$4^6 =$ _____

$4^5 =$ _____

$4^4 =$ _____

$4^3 =$ _____

$4^2 =$ _____

$4^1 =$ _____

Study the patterns for a, b, and c above. Then answer the questions.

1. Describe the pattern of the exponents from the top of each column to the bottom.

2. Describe the pattern of the powers from the top of the column to the bottom.

3. What would you expect the following powers to be?

2^0 5^0 4^0

4. Write a rule. Test it on patterns that you obtain using -2, -5, and -4 as bases.

Study the pattern below. Then answer the questions.

$0^3 = 0$ $0^2 = 0$ $0^1 = 0$ $0^0 =$ _____?_____ 0^{-1} does not exist.
0^{-2} does not exist. 0^{-3} does not exist.

5. Why do 0^{-1}, 0^{-2}, and 0^{-3} not exist?

6. Based upon the pattern, can you determine whether 0^0 exists?

7. The symbol 0^0 is called an **indeterminate,** which means that it has no unique value. Thus it does not exist as a unique real number. Why do you think that 0^0 cannot equal 1?

Patterns with Powers

Use your calculator, if necessary, to complete each pattern.

a. $2^{10} =$	**1024**	**b.** $5^{10} =$	**9,765,625**	**c.** $4^{10} =$	**1,048,576**
$2^9 =$	**512**	$5^9 =$	**1,953,125**	$4^9 =$	**262,144**
$2^8 =$	**256**	$5^8 =$	**390,625**	$4^8 =$	**65,536**
$2^7 =$	**128**	$5^7 =$	**78,125**	$4^7 =$	**16,384**
$2^6 =$	**64**	$5^6 =$	**15,625**	$4^6 =$	**4096**
$2^5 =$	**32**	$5^5 =$	**3125**	$4^5 =$	**1024**
$2^4 =$	**16**	$5^4 =$	**625**	$4^4 =$	**256**
$2^3 =$	**8**	$5^3 =$	**125**	$4^3 =$	**64**
$2^2 =$	**4**	$5^2 =$	**25**	$4^2 =$	**16**
$2^1 =$	**2**	$5^1 =$	**5**	$4^1 =$	**4**

Study the patterns for a, b, and c above. Then answer the questions.

1. Describe the pattern of the exponents from the top of each column to the bottom.
The exponents decrease by one from each row to the one below.

2. Describe the pattern of the powers from the top of the column to the bottom. **To get each power, divide the power on the row above by the base (2, 5, or 4).**

3. What would you expect the following powers to be?

2^0 **1** $\qquad$ 5^0 **1** $\qquad$ 4^0 **1**

4. Write a rule. Test it on patterns that you obtain using $-2, -5,$ and -4 as bases. **Any nonzero number to the zero power equals 1.**

Study the pattern below. Then answer the questions.

$0^3 = 0$ $\quad$ $0^2 = 0$ $\quad$ $0^1 = 0$ $\quad$ $0^0 =$ ___?___ $\quad$ 0^{-1} does not exist.
0^{-2} does not exist. $\quad$ 0^{-3} does not exist.

5. Why do $0^{-1}, 0^{-2},$ and 0^{-3} not exist?
Negative exponents are not defined unless the base is nonzero.

6. Based upon the pattern, can you determine whether 0^0 exists?
No, since the pattern $0^n = 0$ breaks down for $n < 1$.

7. The symbol 0^0 is called an **indeterminate**, which means that it has no unique value. Thus it does not exist as a unique real number. Why do you think that 0^0 cannot equal 1? **Sample answer:**
If $0^0 = 1$, then $1 = \dfrac{1}{1} = \dfrac{1^0}{0^0} = \left(\dfrac{1}{0}\right)^0$, which is a false result, since division by zero is not allowed. Thus, 0^0 cannot equal 1.

8-2

Enrichment

Student Edition
Pages 341–346

The Four Digits Problem

One well-known problem in mathematics is to write expressions for consecutive numbers from 1 upward as far as possible. On this page, you will use the digits 1, 2, 3, and 4. Each digit is used only once. You can use addition, subtraction, multiplication (not division), exponents, and parentheses in any way you wish. Also, you can use two digits to make one number, as in 12 or 34.

Express each number as a combination of the digits 1, 2, 3, and 4.

$1 = (3 \times 1) - (4 - 2)$

$2 = $ _____

$3 = $ _____

$4 = $ _____

$5 = $ _____

$6 = $ _____

$7 = $ _____

$8 = $ _____

$9 = $ _____

$10 = $ _____

$11 = $ _____

$12 = $ _____

$13 = $ _____

$14 = $ _____

$15 = $ _____

$16 = $ _____

$17 = $ _____

$18 = $ _____

$19 = 3(2 + 4) + 1$

$20 = $ _____

$21 = $ _____

$22 = $ _____

$23 = 31 - (4 \times 2)$

$24 = $ _____

$25 = $ _____

$26 = $ _____

$27 = $ _____

$28 = $ _____

$29 = $ _____

$30 = $ _____

$31 = $ _____

$32 = $ _____

$33 = $ _____

$34 = $ _____

$35 = 2^{(4+1)} + 3$

$36 = $ _____

$37 = $ _____

$38 = $ _____

$39 = $ _____

$40 = $ _____

$41 = $ _____

$42 = $ _____

$43 = 42 + 1^3$

$44 = $ _____

$45 = $ _____

$46 = $ _____

$47 = $ _____

$48 = $ _____

$49 = $ _____

$50 = $ _____

Does a calculator help in solving these types of puzzles? Give reasons for your opinion.

_____

_____

_____

NAME _____ DATE _____ PERIOD _____

Enrichment

The Four Digits Problem

One well-known problem in mathematics is to write expressions for consecutive numbers from 1 upward as far as possible. On this page, you will use the digits 1, 2, 3, and 4. Each digit is used only once. You can use addition, subtraction, multiplication (not division), exponents, and parentheses in any way you wish. Also, you can use two digits to make one number, as in 12 or 34.

Sample answers are given.

Express each number as a combination of the digits 1, 2, 3, and 4.

$1 = (3 \times 1) - (4 - 2)$

$2 = (4 - 3) + (2 - 1)$

$3 = (4 - 3) + (2 \times 1)$

$4 = (4 - 2) + (3 - 1)$

$5 = (4 - 2) + (3 \times 1)$

$6 = 4 + 3 + 1 - 2$

$7 = 3(4 - 1) - 2$

$8 = 4 + 3 + 2 - 1$

$9 = 4 + 2 + (3 \times 1)$

$10 = 4 + 3 + 2 + 1$

$11 = (4 \times 3) - (2 - 1)$

$12 = (4 \times 3) \times (2 - 1)$

$13 = (4 \times 3) + (2 - 1)$

$14 = (4 \times 3) + (2 \times 1)$

$15 = 2(3 + 4) + 1$

$16 = (4 \times 2) \times (3 - 1)$

$17 = 3(2 + 4) - 1$

$18 = (2 \times 3) \times (4 - 1)$

$19 = 3(2 + 4) + 1$

$20 = 21 - (4 - 3)$

$21 = (4 + 3) \times (2 + 1)$

$22 = 21 + (4 - 3)$

$23 = 31 - (4 \times 2)$

$24 = (2 + 4) \times (3 + 1)$

$25 = (2 + 3) \times (4 + 1)$

$26 = 24 + (3 - 1)$

$27 = 3^2 \times (4 - 1)$

$28 = 21 + 3 + 4$

$29 = 2^{(4+1)} - 3$

$30 = (2 \times 3) \times (4 + 1)$

$31 = 34 - (2 + 1)$

$32 = 4^2 \times (3 - 1)$

$33 = 21 + (3 \times 4)$

$34 = 2 \times (14 + 3)$

$35 = 2^{(4+1)} + 3$

$36 = 34 + (2 \times 1)$

$37 = 31 + 2 + 4$

$38 = 42 - (3 + 1)$

$39 = 42 - (3 \times 1)$

$40 = 41 - (3 - 2)$

$41 = 43 - (2 \times 1)$

$42 = 43 - (2 - 1)$

$43 = 42 + 1^3$

$44 = 43 + (2 - 1)$

$45 = 43 + (2 \times 1)$

$46 = 43 + (2 + 1)$

$47 = 31 + 4^2$

$48 = 4^2 \times (3 \times 1)$

$49 = 41 + 2^3$

$50 = 41 + 3^2$

Does a calculator help in solving these types of puzzles? Give reasons for your opinion.

See students' work.

Algebra: Concepts and Applications

8-3

Enrichment

Student Edition
Pages 347–351

Rational Exponents

You have developed the following properties of powers when a is a positive real number and m and n are integers.

$$a^m \cdot a^n = a^{m+n} \qquad (ab)^m = a^m b^m \qquad a^0 = 1$$

$$(a^m)^n = a^{mn} \qquad \frac{a^m}{a^n} = a^{m-n} \qquad a^{-m} = \frac{1}{a^m}$$

Exponents need not be restricted to integers. We can define rational exponents so that operations involving them will be governed by the properties for integer exponents.

$$\left(a^{\frac{1}{2}}\right)^2 = a^{\frac{1}{2} \cdot 2} = a \qquad \left(a^{\frac{1}{3}}\right)^3 = a^{\frac{1}{3} \cdot 3} \qquad \left(a^{\frac{1}{n}}\right)^n = a^{\frac{1}{n} \cdot n} = a$$

$a^{\frac{1}{2}}$ squared is a. $\qquad$ $a^{\frac{1}{3}}$ cubed is a. $\qquad$ $a^{\frac{1}{n}}$ to the n power is a.

$a^{\frac{1}{2}}$ is a square root of a. $\quad$ $a^{\frac{1}{3}}$ is a cube root of a. $\quad$ $a^{\frac{1}{n}}$ is an nth root of a.

$$a^{\frac{1}{2}} = \sqrt{a} \qquad\qquad a^{\frac{1}{3}} = \sqrt[3]{a} \qquad\qquad a^{\frac{1}{n}} = \sqrt[n]{a}$$

Now let us investigate the meaning of $a^{\frac{m}{n}}$.

$$a^{\frac{m}{n}} = a^{m \cdot \frac{1}{n}} (a^m)^{\frac{1}{n}} = \sqrt[n]{a^m} \qquad\qquad a^{\frac{m}{n}} = a^{\frac{1}{n} \cdot m} = \left(a^{\frac{1}{n}}\right)^m = (\sqrt[n]{a})^m$$

Therefore, $a^{\frac{m}{n}} = \sqrt[n]{a^m}$ or $(\sqrt[n]{a})^m$.

Example 1: Write $\sqrt[4]{a^3}$ in exponential form. $\qquad$ **Example 2:** Write $a^{\frac{2}{5}}$ in radical form.

$$\sqrt[4]{a^3} = a^{\frac{3}{4}} \qquad\qquad\qquad\qquad\qquad a^{\frac{2}{5}} = \sqrt[5]{a^2}$$

Example 3: Find $\dfrac{a^{\frac{2}{3}}}{a^{\frac{1}{2}}}$.

$$\frac{a^{\frac{2}{3}}}{a^{\frac{1}{2}}} = a^{\frac{2}{3} - \frac{1}{2}} = a^{\frac{4}{6} - \frac{3}{6}} = a^{\frac{1}{6}} \text{ or } \sqrt[6]{a}$$

Write each expression in radical form.

1. $b^{\frac{3}{2}}$ $\qquad\qquad\qquad$ 2. $3c^{\frac{1}{2}}$ $\qquad\qquad\qquad$ 3. $(3c)^{\frac{1}{2}}$

Write each expression in exponential form.

4. $\sqrt[3]{b^4}$ $\qquad\qquad\qquad$ 5. $\sqrt{4a^3}$ $\qquad\qquad\qquad$ 6. $2 \cdot \sqrt[3]{b^2}$

Perform the operation indicated. Answers should show positive exponents only.

7. $\left(a^3 b^{\frac{1}{4}}\right)^2$ $\qquad\qquad$ 8. $\dfrac{-8a^{\frac{3}{4}}}{2a^{\frac{1}{2}}}$ $\qquad\qquad$ 9. $\left(\dfrac{b^{\frac{1}{2}}}{b^{-\frac{2}{3}}}\right)^3$

10. $\sqrt{a^3} \cdot \sqrt{a}$ $\qquad\qquad$ 11. $\left(a^2 b^{-\frac{1}{3}}\right)^{-\frac{1}{2}}$ $\qquad\qquad$ 12. $-2a^{\frac{1}{3}} b^0 \left(5a^{\frac{1}{2}} b^{-\frac{2}{3}}\right)$

Enrichment

Rational Exponents

You have developed the following properties of powers when a
is a positive real number and m and n are integers.

$$a^m \cdot a^n = a^{m+n} \qquad (ab)^m = a^m b^m \qquad a^0 = 1$$

$$(a^m)^n = a^{mn} \qquad \frac{a^m}{a^n} = a^{m-n} \qquad a^{-m} = \frac{1}{a^m}$$

Exponents need not be restricted to integers. We can define
rational exponents so that operations involving them will be
governed by the properties for integer exponents.

$$\left(a^{\frac{1}{2}}\right)^2 = a^{\frac{1}{2} \cdot 2} = a \qquad \left(a^{\frac{1}{3}}\right)^3 = a^{\frac{1}{3} \cdot 3} \qquad \left(a^{\frac{1}{n}}\right)^n = a^{\frac{1}{n} \cdot n} = a$$

$a^{\frac{1}{2}}$ squared is a. $\qquad$ $a^{\frac{1}{3}}$ cubed is a. $\qquad$ $a^{\frac{1}{n}}$ to the n power is a.

$a^{\frac{1}{2}}$ is a square root of a. $\quad$ $a^{\frac{1}{3}}$ is a cube root of a. $\quad$ $a^{\frac{1}{n}}$ is an nth root of a.

$$a^{\frac{1}{2}} = \sqrt{a} \qquad a^{\frac{1}{3}} = \sqrt[3]{a} \qquad a^{\frac{1}{n}} = \sqrt[n]{a}$$

Now let us investigate the meaning of $a^{\frac{m}{n}}$.

$$a^{\frac{m}{n}} = a^{m \cdot \frac{1}{n}} (a^m)^{\frac{1}{n}} = \sqrt[n]{a^m} \qquad\qquad a^{\frac{m}{n}} = a^{\frac{1}{n} \cdot m} = \left(a^{\frac{1}{n}}\right)^m = (\sqrt[n]{a})^m$$

Therefore, $a^{\frac{m}{n}} = \sqrt[n]{a^m}$ or $(\sqrt[n]{a})^m$.

Example 1: Write $\sqrt[4]{a^3}$ in exponential form. $\qquad$ **Example 2:** Write $a^{\frac{2}{5}}$ in radical form.

$$\sqrt[4]{a^3} = a^{\frac{3}{4}} \qquad\qquad\qquad\qquad a^{\frac{2}{5}} = \sqrt[5]{a^2}$$

Example 3: Find $\dfrac{a^{\frac{2}{3}}}{a^{\frac{1}{2}}}$.

$$\frac{a^{\frac{2}{3}}}{a^{\frac{1}{2}}} = a^{\frac{2}{3} - \frac{1}{2}} = a^{\frac{4}{6} - \frac{3}{6}} = a^{\frac{1}{6}} \text{ or } \sqrt[6]{a}$$

Write each expression in radical form.

1. $b^{\frac{3}{2}}$ $\quad$ **$\sqrt{b^3}$** $\qquad\qquad$ 2. $3c^{\frac{1}{2}}$ $\quad$ **$3\sqrt{c}$** $\qquad\qquad$ 3. $(3c)^{\frac{1}{2}}$ $\quad$ **$\sqrt{3c}$**

Write each expression in exponential form.

4. $\sqrt[3]{b^4}$ $\quad$ **$b^{\frac{4}{3}}$** $\qquad$ 5. $\sqrt{4a^3}$ $\quad$ **$(4a^3)^{\frac{1}{2}} = 2a^{\frac{3}{2}}$** $\qquad$ 6. $2 \cdot \sqrt[3]{b^2}$ $\quad$ **$2b^{\frac{2}{3}}$**

**Perform the operation indicated. Answers should show
positive exponents only.**

7. $\left(a^3 b^{\frac{1}{4}}\right)^2$ $\quad$ **$a^6 b^{\frac{1}{2}}$** $\qquad$ 8. $\dfrac{-8a^{\frac{3}{4}}}{2a^{\frac{1}{2}}}$ $\quad$ **$-4a^{\frac{1}{4}}$** $\qquad$ 9. $\left(\dfrac{b^{\frac{1}{2}}}{b^{-\frac{2}{3}}}\right)^3$ $\quad$ **$b^{\frac{7}{2}}$**

10. $\sqrt{a^3} \cdot \sqrt{a}$ $\quad$ **a^2** $\qquad$ 11. $\left(a^2 b^{-\frac{1}{3}}\right)^{-\frac{1}{2}}$ $\quad$ **$\dfrac{b^{\frac{1}{6}}}{a}$** $\qquad$ 12. $-2a^{\frac{1}{3}} b^0 \left(5a^{\frac{1}{2}} b^{-\frac{2}{3}}\right)$ $\quad$ **$\dfrac{-10a^{\frac{5}{6}}}{b^{\frac{2}{3}}}$**

Converting Metric Units

Scientific notation is convenient to use for unit conversions in the metric system.

Example 1: How many kilometers are there in 4,300,000 meters?

Divide the measure by the number of meters (1000) in one kilometer. Express both numbers in scientific notation.

$$\frac{4.3 \times 10^6}{1 \times 10^3} = 4.3 \times 10^3 \qquad \text{The answer is } 4.3 \times 10^3 \text{ km.}$$

Example 2: Convert 3700 grams into milligrams.

Multiply by the number of milligrams (1000) in 1 gram.

$$(3.7 \times 10^3)(1 \times 10^3) = 3.7 \times 10^6 \qquad \text{There are } 3.7 \times 10^6 \text{ mg in 3700 g.}$$

Complete the following. Express each answer in scientific notation.

1. 250,000 m = _____ km

2. 375 km = _____ m

3. 247 m = _____ cm

4. 5000 m = _____ mm

5. 0.0004 km = _____ m

6. 0.01 mm = _____ m

7. 6000 m = _____ mm

8. 340 cm = _____ km

9. 52,000 mg = _____ g

10. 420 kL = _____ L

Solve.

11. The planet Mars has a diameter of 6.76×10^3 km. What is the diameter of Mars in meters? Express the answer in both scientific and decimal notation.

12. The distance of the earth from the sun is 149,590,000 km. Light travels 3.0×10^8 meters per second. How long does it take light from the sun to reach the earth in minutes?

13. A light-year is the distance that light travels in one year. (See Exercise 12.) How far is a light year in kilometers? Express your answer in scientific notation.

Converting Metric Units

Scientific notation is convenient to use for unit conversions in the metric system.

Example 1: How many kilometers are there in 4,300,000 meters?

Divide the measure by the number of meters (1000) in one kilometer. Express both numbers in scientific notation.

$$\frac{4.3 \times 10^6}{1 \times 10^3} = 4.3 \times 10^3 \qquad \text{The answer is } 4.3 \times 10^3 \text{ km.}$$

Example 2: Convert 3700 grams into milligrams.

Multiply by the number of milligrams (1000) in 1 gram.

$$(3.7 \times 10^3)(1 \times 10^3) = 3.7 \times 10^6 \qquad \text{There are } 3.7 \times 10^6 \text{ mg in 3700 g.}$$

Complete the following. Express each answer in scientific notation.

1. 250,000 m = ___**2.5×10^2**___ km

2. 375 km = ___**3.75×10^5**___ m

3. 247 m = ___**2.47×10^4**___ cm

4. 5000 m = ___**5.0×10^6**___ mm

5. 0.0004 km = ___**4.0×10^{-1}**___ m

6. 0.01 mm = ___**1.0×10^{-5}**___ m

7. 6000 m = ___**6×10^{-6}**___ mm

8. 340 cm = ___**3.4×10^{-3}**___ km

9. 52,000 mg = ___**5.2×10^1**___ g

10. 420 kL = ___**4.2×10^5**___ L

Solve.

11. The planet Mars has a diameter of 6.76×10^3 km. What is the diameter of Mars in meters? Express the answer in both scientific and decimal notation.
6,760,000 m; 6.76×10^6 m

12. The distance of the earth from the sun is 149,590,000 km. Light travels 3.0×10^8 meters per second. How long does it take light from the sun to reach the earth in minutes?
8.31 min

13. A light-year is the distance that light travels in one year. (See Exercise 12.) How far is a light year in kilometers? Express your answer in scientific notation.
9.46×10^{12} km

Enrichment

Standard Deviation

The most commonly used measure of variation is called the
standard deviation. It shows how far the data are from their
mean. You can find the standard deviation using the steps
given below.

a. Find the mean of the data.
b. Find the difference between each value and the mean.
c. Square each difference.
d. Find the mean of the squared differences.
e. Find the square root of the mean found in Step d. The result
   is the standard deviation.

Example: Calculate the standard deviation of the test scores
82, 71, 63, 78, and 66.

$$\text{mean of the data } (m) = \frac{82 + 71 + 63 + 78 + 66}{5} = \frac{360}{5} = 72$$

x	$x - m$	$(x - m)^2$
82	$82 - 72 = 10$	$10^2 = 100$
71	$71 - 72 = -1$	$(-1)^2 = 1$
63	$63 - 72 = -9$	$(-9)^2 = 81$
78	$78 - 72 = 6$	$6^2 = 36$
66	$66 - 72 = -6$	$(-6)^2 = 36$

$$\text{mean of the squared differences} = \frac{100 + 1 + 81 + 36 + 36}{5} = \frac{254}{5} = 50.8$$

$$\text{standard deviation} = \sqrt{50.8} \approx 7.13$$

**Use the test scores 94, 48, 83, 61, and 74 to complete
Exercises 1–3.**

1. Find the mean of the scores.

2. Show that the standard deviation of the scores is about 16.2.

3. Which had less variations, the test scores listed above or the
   test scores in the example?

Standard Deviation

The most commonly used measure of variation is called the
standard deviation. It shows how far the data are from their
mean. You can find the standard deviation using the steps
given below.
a. Find the mean of the data.
b. Find the difference between each value and the mean.
c. Square each difference.
d. Find the mean of the squared differences.
e. Find the square root of the mean found in Step d. The result
   is the standard deviation.

Example: Calculate the standard deviation of the test scores
82, 71, 63, 78, and 66.

$$\text{mean of the data } (m) = \frac{82 + 71 + 63 + 78 + 66}{5} = \frac{360}{5} = 72$$

x	$x - m$	$(x - m)^2$
82	$82 - 72 = 10$	$10^2 = 100$
71	$71 - 72 = -1$	$(-1)^2 = 1$
63	$63 - 72 = -9$	$(-9)^2 = 81$
78	$78 - 72 = 6$	$6^2 = 36$
66	$66 - 72 = -6$	$(-6)^2 = 36$

$$\text{mean of the squared differences} = \frac{100 + 1 + 81 + 36 + 36}{5} = \frac{254}{5} = 50.8$$

$$\text{standard deviation} = \sqrt{50.8} \approx 7.13$$

**Use the test scores 94, 48, 83, 61, and 74 to complete
Exercises 1–3.**

1. Find the mean of the scores. **72**

2. Show that the standard deviation of the scores is about 16.2.

x	$x - m$	$(x - m)^2$
94	$94 - 72 = 22$	484
48	$48 - 72 = -24$	576
83	$83 - 72 = 11$	121
61	$61 - 72 = -11$	121
74	$74 - 72 = 2$	4

mean of $(x - m)^2 = 261.2$
S.D. $= \sqrt{261.2} \approx 16.2$

3. Which had less variations, the test scores listed above or the
   test scores in the example? **the test scores in the example**

NAME _____ DATE _____ PERIOD _____

Enrichment

Squares and Square Roots From a Graph

The graph of $y = x^2$ can be used to find the squares and square roots of numbers.

To find the square of 3, locate 3 on the x-axis. Then find its corresponding value on the y-axis.

The arrows show that $3^2 = 9$.

To find the square root of 4, first locate 4 on the y-axis. Then find its corresponding value on the x-axis. Following the arrows on the graph, you can see that $\sqrt{4} = 2$.

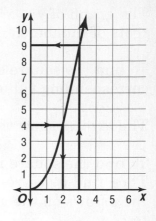

A small part of the graph at $y = x^2$ is shown below. A 1:10 ratio for unit length on the y-axis to unit length on the x-axis is used.

Example: Find $\sqrt{11}$.

The arrows show that $\sqrt{11} = 3.3$ to the nearest tenth.

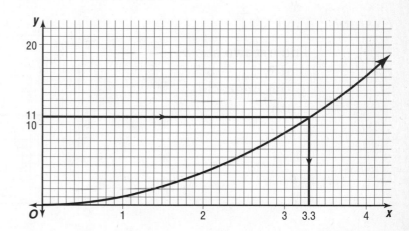

Use the graph above to find each of the following to the nearest whole number.

1. 1.5^2 **2.** 2.7^2 **3.** 0.9^2

4. 3.6^2 **5.** 4.2^2 **6.** 3.9^2

Use the graph above to find each of the following to the nearest tenth.

7. $\sqrt{15}$ **8.** $\sqrt{8}$ **9.** $\sqrt{3}$

10. $\sqrt{5}$ **11.** $\sqrt{14}$ **12.** $\sqrt{17}$

Algebra: Concepts and Applications

Enrichment

Squares and Square Roots From a Graph

The graph of $y = x^2$ can be used to find the squares and square roots of numbers.

To find the square of 3, locate 3 on the x-axis. Then find its corresponding value on the y-axis.

The arrows show that $3^2 = 9$.

To find the square root of 4, first locate 4 on the y-axis. Then find its corresponding value on the x-axis. Following the arrows on the graph, you can see that $\sqrt{4} = 2$.

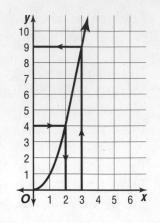

A small part of the graph at $y = x^2$ is shown below. A 1:10 ratio for unit length on the y-axis to unit length on the x-axis is used.

Example: Find $\sqrt{11}$.

The arrows show that $\sqrt{11} = 3.3$ to the nearest tenth.

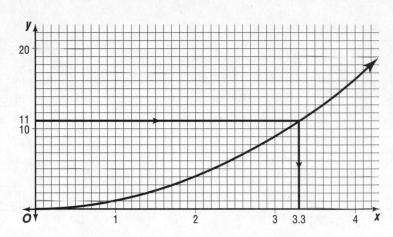

Use the graph above to find each of the following to the nearest whole number.

1. 1.5^2 **2**

2. 2.7^2 **7**

3. 0.9^2 **1**

4. 3.6^2 **13**

5. 4.2^2 **18**

6. 3.9^2 **15**

Use the graph above to find each of the following to the nearest tenth.

7. $\sqrt{15}$ **3.9**

8. $\sqrt{8}$ **2.8**

9. $\sqrt{3}$ **1.7**

10. $\sqrt{5}$ **2.2**

11. $\sqrt{14}$ **3.7**

12. $\sqrt{17}$ **4.1**

Algebra: Concepts and Applications

8-7

Enrichment

Pythagorean Triples

Recall the Pythagorean Theorem.
In a right triangle, the square of the length of the
hypotenuse is equal to the sum of the squares of the
lengths of the legs.

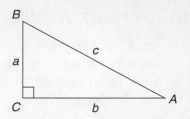

$a^2 + b^2 = c^2$
Note that c is the length
of the hypotenuse.

The integers 3, 4, and 5 satisfy the
Pythagorean Theorem and can be the
lengths of the sides of a right triangle.

$3^2 + 4^2 = 5^2$
$9 + 16 = 25$
$25 = 25$

Furthermore, for any positive integer n,
the numbers $3n$, $4n$, and $5n$ satisfy the
Pythagorean Theorem.

For $n = 2$: $6^2 + 8^2 = 10^2$
$36 + 64 = 100$
$100 = 100$

If three numbers satisfy the Pythagorean Theorem, they are
called a **Pythagorean triple.** Here is an easy way to find other
Pythagorean triples.

The numbers a, b, and c are a Pythagorean triple if
$a = m^2 - n^2$, $b = 2mn$, and $c = m^2 + n^2$,
where m and n are relatively prime positive integers and $m > n$.

Example: Choose $m = 5$ and $n = 2$.

$a = m^2 - n^2$	$b = 2mn$	$c = m^2 + n^2$	**Check:** $20^2 + 21^2 = 29^2$
$= 5^2 - 2^2$	$= 2(5)(2)$	$= 5^2 + 2^2$	$400 + 441 = 841$
$= 25 - 4$	$= 20$	$= 25 + 4$	$841 = 841$
$= 21$		$= 29$	

**Use the following values of m and n to find Pythagorean
triples.**

1. $m = 3$ and $n = 2$ **2.** $m = 4$ *and* $n = 1$ **3.** $m = 5$ and $n = 3$

4. $m = 6$ and $n = 5$ **5.** $m = 10$ and $n = 7$ **6.** $m = 8$ and $n = 5$

Pythagorean Triples

Recall the Pythagorean Theorem.
In a right triangle, the square of the length of the hypotenuse is equal to the sum of the squares of the lengths of the legs.

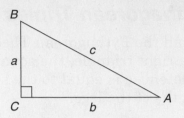

$$a^2 + b^2 = c^2$$
Note that c is the length of the hypotenuse.

The integers 3, 4, and 5 satisfy the Pythagorean Theorem and can be the lengths of the sides of a right triangle.

$$3^2 + 4^2 = 5^2$$
$$9 + 16 = 25$$
$$25 = 25$$

Furthermore, for any positive integer n, the numbers $3n$, $4n$, and $5n$ satisfy the Pythagorean Theorem.

For $n = 2$: $6^2 + 8^2 = 10^2$
$$36 + 64 = 100$$
$$100 = 100$$

If three numbers satisfy the Pythagorean Theorem, they are called a **Pythagorean triple.** Here is an easy way to find other Pythagorean triples.

The numbers a, b, and c are a Pythagorean triple if
$a = m^2 - n^2$, $b = 2mn$, and $c = m^2 + n^2$,
where m and n are relatively prime positive integers and $m > n$.

Example: Choose $m = 5$ and $n = 2$.

$a = m^2 - n^2$	$b = 2mn$	$c = m^2 + n^2$	**Check:** $20^2 + 21^2 = 29^2$
$= 5^2 - 2^2$	$= 2(5)(2)$	$= 5^2 + 2^2$	$400 + 441 = 841$
$= 25 - 4$	$= 20$	$= 25 + 4$	$841 = 841$
$= 21$		$= 29$	

Use the following values of m and n to find Pythagorean triples.

1. $m = 3$ and $n = 2$
   12, 5, 13

2. $m = 4$ and $n = 1$
   8, 15, 17

3. $m = 5$ and $n = 3$
   30, 16, 34

4. $m = 6$ and $n = 5$
   60, 11, 61

5. $m = 10$ and $n = 7$
   140, 51, 149

6. $m = 8$ and $n = 5$
   80, 39, 89

Polynomials and Volume

The volume of a rectangular prism can be written as the product of three polynomials. Recall that the volume equals the length times the width times the height.

The two volumes at the right represent the cube of y and the cube of x.

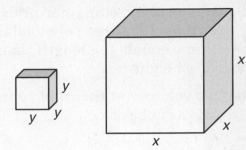

Multiply to find the volume of each prism. Write each answer as an algebraic expression.

1.

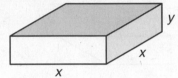

2.

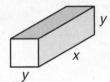

3.

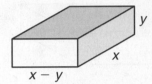

4.

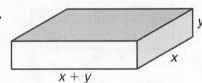

5.

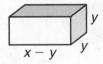

6.

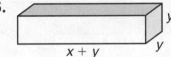

Multiply, then add to find each volume. Write the answer as an algebraic expression.

7.

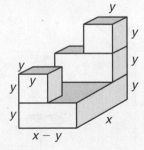

8.

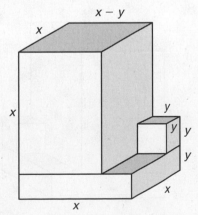

9.

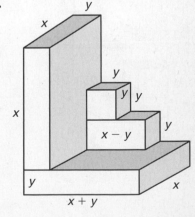

9–1

Enrichment

Polynomials and Volume

The volume of a rectangular prism can be written as the product of three polynomials. Recall that the volume equals the length times the width times the height.

The two volumes at the right represent the cube of y and the cube of x.

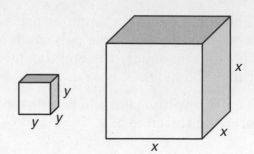

Multiply to find the volume of each prism. Write each answer as an algebraic expression.

1.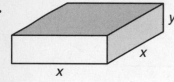

$$x^2y$$

2.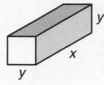

$$xy^2$$

3.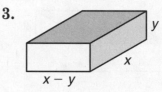

$$xy(x - y)$$

4.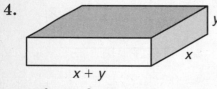

$$xy(x + y)$$

5.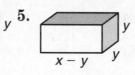

$$y^2(x - y)$$

6.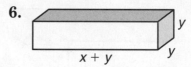

$$y^2(x + y)$$

Multiply, then add to find each volume. Write the answer as an algebraic expression. **Sample answers are given.**

7.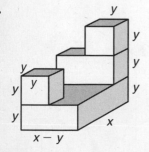

$$2y^3 + y^2(x - y) + \\ xy(x - y)$$

8.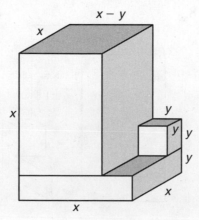

$$x^2(x - y) + \\ y^3 + x^2y$$

9.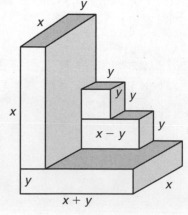

$$x^2y + y^3 + y^2(x - y) + \\ xy(x + y)$$

Algebra: Concepts and Applications

Enrichment

Geometric Series

The terms of this polynomial form a geometric series.

$$a + ar + ar^2 + ar^3 + ar^4$$

The first term is the constant a. Then each term after that is found by multiplying by a constant multiplier r.

Use the equation $S = a + ar + ar^2 + ar^3 + ar^4$ for Exercises 1–3.

1. Multiply each side of the equation by r.

2. Subtract the original equation from your result in Exercise 1.

3. Solve the result from Exercise 2 for the variable S.

Use the polynomial $a + ar + ar^2 + ar^3 + ar^4 + \cdots + ar^{n-1}$ for Exercises 4–8.

4. Write the 10th term of the polynomial.

5. If $a = 5$ and $r = 2$, what is the 8th term?

6. Follow the steps in Exercises 1–3 to write a formula for the sum of this polynomial.

7. If the 3rd term is 20 and the 6th term is 160, solve for r^3 and then find r. Then solve $ar^2 = 20$ for a and find the value of the first six terms of the polynomial.

8. Find the sum of the first six terms of the geometric series that begins 3, 6, 12, 24, $\cdots$. First write the values for a and r.

Geometric Series

The terms of this polynomial form a geometric series.

$$a + ar + ar^2 + ar^3 + ar^4$$

The first term is the constant a. Then each term after that is found by multiplying by a constant multiplier r.

Use the equation $S = a + ar + ar^2 + ar^3 + ar^4$ for Exercises 1–3.

1. Multiply each side of the equation by r.
   $$rS = ar + ar^2 + ar^3 + ar^4 + ar^5$$

2. Subtract the original equation from your result in Exercise 1.
   $$rS - S = ar^5 - a$$

3. Solve the result from Exercise 2 for the variable S. $S = \dfrac{a(r^5 - 1)}{r - 1}$

Use the polynomial $a + ar + ar^2 + ar^3 + ar^4 + \cdots + ar^{n-1}$ for Exercises 4–8.

4. Write the 10th term of the polynomial. ar^9

5. If $a = 5$ and $r = 2$, what is the 8th term? $ar^7 = 640$

6. Follow the steps in Exercises 1–3 to write a formula for the sum of this polynomial. $S = \dfrac{a(r^n - 1)}{r - 1}$

7. If the 3rd term is 20 and the 6th term is 160, solve for r^3 and then find r. Then solve $ar^2 = 20$ for a and find the value of the first six terms of the polynomial.
   $\dfrac{ar^5}{ar^2} = \dfrac{160}{20}$, $r^3 = 8$, $r = 2$; $ar^2 = 20$; $a = 5$; 5, 10, 20, 40, 80, 160

8. Find the sum of the first six terms of the geometric series that begins 3, 6, 12, 24, $\cdots$. First write the values for a and r.
   $a = 3, r = 2$
   $$S = \frac{3(2^6 - 1)}{2 - 1} = 3 \times 63 = 189$$

NAME _____ DATE _____ PERIOD _____

Enrichment

Student Edition
Pages 394–398

Circular Areas and Volumes

Area of Circle	Volume of Cylinder	Volume of Cone
$A = \pi r^2$	$V = \pi r^2 h$	$V = \frac{1}{3}\pi r^2 h$

 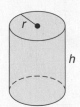 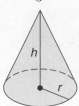

Write an algebraic expression for each shaded area. (Recall that the diameter of a circle is twice its radius.)

1.
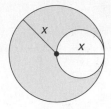

2.
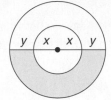

3.
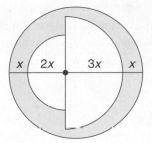

Write an algebraic expression of the total volume of each figure.

4.
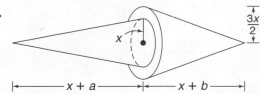

5.

Each figure has a cylindrical hole with a radius of 2 inches and a height of 5 inches. Find each volume.

6.
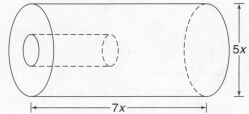

7.
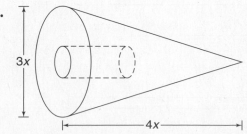

57

Algebra: Concepts and Applications

Circular Areas and Volumes

Area of Circle	Volume of Cylinder	Volume of Cone
$A = \pi r^2$	$V = \pi r^2 h$	$V = \frac{1}{3}\pi r^2 h$

 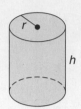 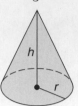

Write an algebraic expression for each shaded area. (Recall that the diameter of a circle is twice its radius.)

1.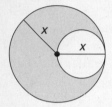

2.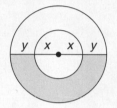

3.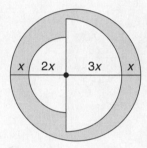

$$\pi x^2 - \pi\left(\frac{x}{2}\right)^2 = \frac{3}{4}\pi x^2 \qquad \frac{\pi}{2}(y^2 + 2xy) \qquad \frac{23\pi}{4}x^2$$

Write an algebraic expression of the total volume of each figure.

4.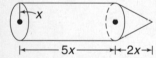

5.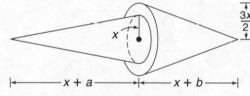

$$5\frac{2}{3}\pi x^3 \qquad\qquad \frac{\pi}{12}[13x^3 + (4a + 9b)x^2]$$

Each figure has a cylindrical hole with a radius of 2 inches and a height of 5 inches. Find each volume.

6.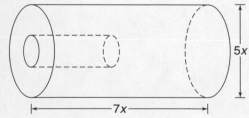

7.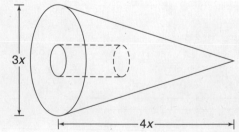

$$\frac{175\pi}{4}x^3 - 20\pi \text{ in}^3 \qquad\qquad 3\pi x^3 - 20\pi \text{ in}^3$$

NAME _____ DATE _____ PERIOD _____

Enrichment

Student Edition
Pages 399–404

Powers of Binomials

This arrangement of numbers is called Pascal's Triangle. It was first published in 1665, but was known hundreds of years earlier.

```
            1
          1   1
        1   2   1
      1   3   3   1
    1   4   6   4   1
```

1. Each number in the triangle is found by adding two numbers. What two numbers were added to get the 6 in the 5th row?

2. Describe how to create the 6th row of Pascal's Triangle.

3. Write the numbers for rows 6 through 10 of the triangle.

   Row 6:

   Row 7:

   Row 8:

   Row 9:

   Row 10:

Multiply to find the expanded form of each product.

4. $(a + b)^2$

5. $(a + b)^3$

6. $(a + b)^4$

Now compare the coefficients of the three products in Exercises 4–6 with Pascal's Triangle.

7. Describe the relationship between the expanded form of $(a + b)^n$ and Pascal's Triangle.

8. Use Pascal's Triangle to write the expanded form of $(a + b)^6$.

9-4

Enrichment

Powers of Binomials

This arrangement of numbers is called Pascal's Triangle. It was first published in 1665, but was known hundreds of years earlier.

```
              1
            1   1
          1   2   1
        1   3   3   1
      1   4   6   4   1
```

1. Each number in the triangle is found by adding two numbers. What two numbers were added to get the 6 in the 5th row?
   3 and 3

2. Describe how to create the 6th row of Pascal's Triangle.
   The first and last numbers are 1. Evaluate 1 + 4, 4 + 6, 6 + 4, and 4 + 1 to find the other numbers.

3. Write the numbers for rows 6 through 10 of the triangle.

   Row 6: **1   5   10   10   5   1**

   Row 7: **1   6   15   20   15   6   1**

   Row 8: **1   7   21   35   35   21   7   1**

   Row 9: **1   8   28   56   70   56   28   8   1**

   Row 10: **1   9   37   84   126   126   84   37   9   1**

Multiply to find the expanded form of each product.

4. $(a + b)^2$ $a^2 + 2ab + b^2$

5. $(a + b)^3$ $a^3 + 3a^2b + 3ab^2 + b^3$

6. $(a + b)^4$ $a^4 + 4a^3b + 6a^2b^2 + 4ab^3 + b^4$

Now compare the coefficients of the three products in Exercises 4–6 with Pascal's Triangle.

7. Describe the relationship between the expanded form of $(a + b)^n$ and Pascal's Triangle. **The coefficients of the expanded form are found in row $n + 1$ of Pascal's Triangle.**

8. Use Pascal's Triangle to write the expanded form of $(a + b)^6$.
   $a^6 + 6a^5b + 15a^4b^2 + 20a^3b^3 + 15a^2b^4 + 6ab^5 + b^6$

9-5

Enrichment

Squaring Numbers: A Shortcut

A shortcut helps you to square a positive two-digit number ending in 5. The method is developed using the idea that a two-digit number may be expressed as $10t + u$. Suppose $u = 5$.

$$(10t + 5)^2 = (10t + 5)(10t + 5)$$
$$= 100t^2 + 50t + 50t + 25$$
$$= 100t^2 + 100t + 25$$
$$(10t + 5)^2 = 100t(t + 1) + 25$$

In words, this formula says that the square of a two-digit number has $t(t + 1)$ in the hundreds place. Then 2 is the tens digit and 5 is the units digit.

Example: Using the formula for $(10t + 5)^2$, find 85^2.
$$85^2 = 100 \cdot 8 \cdot (8 + 1) + 25$$
$$= 7200 + 25$$
$$= 7225 \qquad \textit{Shortcut: First think } 8 \cdot 9 = 72.$$
$$\textit{Then write 25.}$$

Thus, to square a number, such as 85, you can write the product of the tens digit and the next consecutive integer $t + 1$. Then write 25.

Find each of the following using the shortcut.

1. 15^2 2. 25^2 3. 35^2

4. 45^2 5. 55^2 6. 65^2

Solve each problem.

7. What is the tens digit in the square of 95?

8. What are the first two digits in the square of 75?

9. Any three-digit number can be written as $100a + 10b + c$. Square this expression to show that if the last digit of a three-digit number is 5 then the last two digits of the square of the number are 2 and 5.

Squaring Numbers: A Shortcut

A shortcut helps you to square a positive two-digit number ending in 5. The method is developed using the idea that a two-digit number may be expressed as $10t + u$. Suppose $u = 5$.

$$(10t + 5)^2 = (10t + 5)(10t + 5)$$
$$= 100t^2 + 50t + 50t + 25$$
$$= 100t^2 + 100t + 25$$
$$(10t + 5)^2 = 100t(t + 1) + 25$$

In words, this formula says that the square of a two-digit number has $t(t + 1)$ in the hundreds place. Then 2 is the tens digit and 5 is the units digit.

Example: Using the formula for $(10t + 5)^2$, find 85^2.
$$85^2 = 100 \cdot 8 \cdot (8 + 1) + 25$$
$$= 7200 + 25$$
$$= 7225 \qquad \text{Shortcut: First think } 8 \cdot 9 = 72.$$
$$\text{Then write } 25.$$

Thus, to square a number, such as 85, you can write the product of the tens digit and the next consecutive integer $t + 1$. Then write 25.

Find each of the following using the shortcut.

1. 15^2 **225**

2. 25^2 **625**

3. 35^2 **1225**

4. 45^2 **2025**

5. 55^2 **3025**

6. 65^2 **4225**

Solve each problem.

7. What is the tens digit in the square of 95? **2**

8. What are the first two digits in the square of 75? **56**

9. Any three-digit number can be written as $100a + 10b + c$. Square this expression to show that if the last digit of a three-digit number is 5 then the last two digits of the square of the number are 2 and 5.
**$10{,}000a^2 + 2000ab + 200ac + 100b^2 + 20bc + c^2 =$
$10{,}000a^2 + 2000ab + 1000a + 100b^2 + 100b + 25$
The last two digits are not affected by the first five terms.**

10-1

Enrichment

Student Edition
Pages 420–425

Finding the GCF by Euclid's Algorithm

Finding the greatest common factor of two large numbers can take a long time using prime factorizations. This method can be avoided by using **Euclid's Algorithm** as shown in the following example.

Example: Find the GCF of 209 and 532.

Divide the greater number, 532, by the lesser, 209.

$$
\begin{array}{r}
2 \\
209\overline{)532} \\
418 \\
\end{array}
$$

Divide the remainder into the divisor above. Repeat this process until the remainder is zero. The last nonzero remainder is the GCF.

$$
\begin{array}{r}
1 \\
114\overline{)209} \\
114 \\
\end{array}
\qquad
\begin{array}{r}
1 \\
95\overline{)114} \\
95 \\
\end{array}
\qquad
\begin{array}{r}
5 \\
19\overline{)95} \\
95 \\
\hline
0
\end{array}
$$

The divisor, 19, is the GCF of 209 and 532.

Suppose the GCF of two numbers is found to be 1. Then the numbers are said to be **relatively prime.**

Find the GCF of each group of numbers by using Euclid's Algorithm.

1. 187; 578

2. 1802; 106

3. 161; 943

4. 215; 1849

5. 1325; 3498

6. 3484; 5963

7. 33,583; 4257

8. 453; 484

9. 95; 209; 589

10. 518; 407; 851

11. $17a^2x^2z$; $1615axz^2$

12. $752cf^3$; $893c^3f^3$

13. $979r^2s^2$; $495rs^3$, $154r^3s^3$

14. $360x^5y^7$; $328xy$; $568x^3y^3$

Enrichment

Finding the GCF by Euclid's Algorithm

Finding the greatest common factor of two large numbers can take a long time using prime factorizations. This method can be avoided by using **Euclid's Algorithm** as shown in the following example.

Example: Find the GCF of 209 and 532.

Divide the greater number, 532, by the lesser, 209.

$$
\begin{array}{r}
2 \\
209\overline{)532} \\
418
\end{array}
\qquad
\begin{array}{r}
1 \\
114\overline{)209} \\
114
\end{array}
$$

Divide the remainder into the divisor above. Repeat this process until the remainder is zero. The last nonzero remainder is the GCF.

$$
\begin{array}{r}
1 \\
95\overline{)114} \\
95
\end{array}
\qquad
\begin{array}{r}
5 \\
19\overline{)95} \\
95 \\
\hline
0
\end{array}
$$

The divisor, 19, is the GCF of 209 and 532.

Suppose the GCF of two numbers is found to be 1. Then the numbers are said to be **relatively prime.**

Find the GCF of each group of numbers by using Euclid's Algorithm.

1. 187; 578 **17**

2. 1802; 106 **106**

3. 161; 943 **23**

4. 215; 1849 **43**

5. 1325; 3498 **53**

6. 3484; 5963 **67**

7. 33,583; 4257 **473**

8. 453; 484 **1**

9. 95; 209; 589 **19**

10. 518; 407; 851 **37**

11. $17a^2x^2z$; $1615axz^2$ **17axz**

12. $752cf^3$; $893c^3f^3$ **47cf³**

13. $979r^2s^2$; $495rs^3$, $154r^3s^3$ **11rs²**

14. $360x^5y^7$; $328xy$; $568x^3y^3$ **8xy**

Puzzling Primes

A **prime number** has only two factors, itself and 1. The number
6 is not prime because it has 2 and 3 as factors; 5 and 7 are
prime. The number 1 is not considered to be prime.

1. Use a calculator to help you find the 25 prime numbers less
   than 100.

   _____

   _____

Prime numbers have interested mathematicians for centuries.
They have tried to find expressions that will give all the prime
numbers, or only prime numbers. In the 1700s, Euler discovered
that the expression $x^2 + x + 41$ will yield prime numbers for
values of x from 0 through 39.

2. Find the prime numbers generated by Euler's formula for x
   from 0 through 7.

   _____

   _____

3. Show that the expression $x^2 + x + 31$ will not give prime
   numbers for very many values of x.

   _____

   _____

4. Find the largest prime number generated by Euler's formula. _____

Goldbach's Conjecture is that every nonzero even number
greater than 2 can be written as the sum of two primes. No one has
ever proved that this is always true. No one has disproved it, either.

5. Show that Goldbach's Conjecture is true for the first 5 even
   numbers greater than 2.

   _____

   _____

6. Give a way that someone could disprove Goldbach's Conjecture.

   _____

   _____

   _____

Puzzling Primes

A **prime number** has only two factors, itself and 1. The number 6 is not prime because it has 2 and 3 as factors; 5 and 7 are prime. The number 1 is not considered to be prime.

1. Use a calculator to help you find the 25 prime numbers less than 100.

   2, 3, 5, 7, 11, 13, 17, 19, 23, 29, 31, 37 41, 43, 47, 53, 59, 61,

   67, 71, 73, 79, 83, 89, 97

Prime numbers have interested mathematicians for centuries. They have tried to find expressions that will give all the prime numbers, or only prime numbers. In the 1700s, Euler discovered that the expression $x^2 + x + 41$ will yield prime numbers for values of x from 0 through 39.

2. Find the prime numbers generated by Euler's formula for x from 0 through 7.

   41, 43, 47, 53, 61, 71, 83, 97

3. Show that the expression $x^2 + x + 31$ will not give prime numbers for very many values of x.

   It works for x = 0, 2, 3, 5, and 6 but not for x = 1, 4, and 7.

4. Find the largest prime number generated by Euler's formula. _____ **1601** _____

Goldbach's Conjecture is that every nonzero even number greater than 2 can be written as the sum of two primes. No one has ever proved that this is always true. No one has disproved it, either.

5. Show that Goldbach's Conjecture is true for the first 5 even numbers greater than 2.

   4 = 2 + 2, 6 = 3 + 3, 8 = 3 + 5, 10 = 3 + 7, 12 = 5 + 7

6. Give a way that someone could disprove Goldbach's Conjecture.

   Find an even number that cannot be written as the sum of

   two primes.

10-3

Enrichment

Student Edition
Pages 434–439

Area Models for Quadratic Trinomials

After you have factored a quadratic trinomial, you can use the
factors to draw geometric models of the trinomial.

$$x^2 + 5x - 6 = (x - 1)(x + 6)$$

To draw a rectangular model, the value
2 was used for x so that the shorter
side would have a length of 1. Then
the drawing was done in centimeters. So,
the area of the rectangle is $x^2 + 5x - 6$.

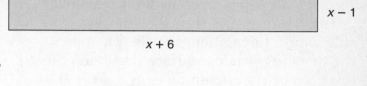

To draw a right triangle model, recall
that the area of a triangle is one-half
the base times the height. So, one of
the sides must be twice as long as the
shorter side of the rectangular model.

$$x^2 + 5x - 6 = (x - 1)(x + 6)$$
$$= \frac{1}{2}(2x - 2)(x + 6)$$

The area of the right triangle is also $x^2 + 5x - 6$.

**Factor each trinomial. Then follow the directions to draw each
model of the trinomial.**

1. $x^2 + 2x - 3$
   Use $x = 2$. Draw a rectangle
   in centimeters.

2. $3x^2 + 5x - 2$
   Use $x = 1$. Draw a rectangle
   in centimeters.

3. $x^2 - 4x + 3$
   Use $x = 4$. Draw two different
   right triangles in centimeters.

4. $9x^2 - 9x + 2$
   Use $x = 2$. Draw two different right triangles.
   Use 0.5 centimeter for each unit.

Area Models for Quadratic Trinomials

After you have factored a quadratic trinomial, you can use the factors to draw geometric models of the trinomial.

$$x^2 + 5x - 6 = (x - 1)(x + 6)$$

To draw a rectangular model, the value 2 was used for x so that the shorter side would have a length of 1. Then the drawing was done in centimeters. So, the area of the rectangle is $x^2 + 5x - 6$.

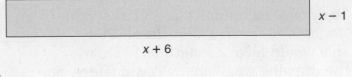

To draw a right triangle model, recall that the area of a triangle is one-half the base times the height. So, one of the sides must be twice as long as the shorter side of the rectangular model.

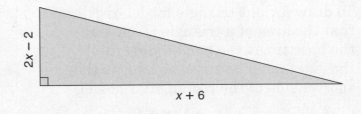

$$x^2 + 5x - 6 = (x - 1)(x + 6)$$
$$= \frac{1}{2}(2x - 2)(x + 6)$$

The area of the right triangle is also $x^2 + 5x - 6$.

Factor each trinomial. Then follow the directions to draw each model of the trinomial.

1. $x^2 + 2x - 3$
   Use $x = 2$. Draw a rectangle
   in centimeters. **(x + 3)(x − 1)**

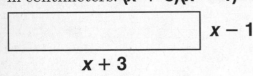

2. $3x^2 + 5x - 2$
   Use $x = 1$. Draw a rectangle
   in centimeters. **(x + 2)(3x − 1)**

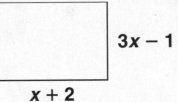

3. $x^2 - 4x + 3$
   Use $x = 4$. Draw two different
   right triangles in centimeters. **(x − 1)(x − 3)**

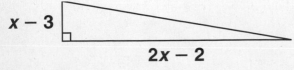

4. $9x^2 - 9x + 2$
   Use $x = 2$. Draw two different right triangles.
   Use 0.5 centimeter for each unit. **(3x − 2)(3x − 1)**

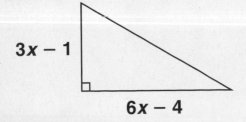

10-4 Enrichment

Student Edition
Pages 440–444

Factoring Trinomials of Fourth Degree

Some trinomials of the form $a^4 + a^2b^2 + b^4$ can be written as the difference of two squares and then factored.

Example: Factor $4x^4 - 37x^2y^2 + 9y^4$.

Step 1 Find the square roots of the first and last terms.

$$\sqrt{4x^4} = 2x^2 \qquad \sqrt{9y^4} = 3y^2$$

Step 2 Find twice the product of the square roots.

$$2(2x^2)(3y^2) = 12x^2y^2$$

Step 3 Separate the middle term into two parts. One part is either your answer to Step 2 or its opposite. The other part should be the opposite of a perfect square.

$$-37x^2y^2 = -12x^2y^2 - 25x^2y^2$$

Step 4 Rewrite the trinomial as the difference of two squares and then factor.

$$
\begin{aligned}
4x^4 - 37x^2y^2 + 9y^4 &= (4x^4 - 12x^2y^2 + 9y^4) - 25x^2y^2 \\
&= (2x^2 - 3y^2)^2 - 25x^2y^2 \\
&= [(2x^2 - 3y^2) + 5xy][(2x^2 - 3y^2) - 5xy] \\
&= (2x^2 + 5xy - 3y^2)(2x^2 - 5xy - 3y^2)
\end{aligned}
$$

Factor each trinomial.

1. $x^4 + x^2y^2 + y^4$

2. $x^4 + x^2 + 1$

3. $9a^4 - 15a^2 + 1$

4. $16a^4 - 17a^2 + 1$

5. $4a^4 - 13a^2 + 1$

6. $9a^4 + 26a^2b^2 + 25b^4$

7. $4x^4 - 21x^2y^2 + 9y^4$

8. $4a^4 - 29a^2c^2 + 25c^4$

10-4

Enrichment

Factoring Trinomials of Fourth Degree

Some trinomials of the form $a^4 + a^2b^2 + b^4$ can be written as the difference of two squares and then factored.

Example: Factor $4x^4 - 37x^2y^2 + 9y^4$.

Step 1 Find the square roots of the first and last terms.

$$\sqrt{4x^4} = 2x^2 \qquad \sqrt{9y^4} = 3y^2$$

Step 2 Find twice the product of the square roots.

$$2(2x^2)(3y^2) = 12x^2y^2$$

Step 3 Separate the middle term into two parts. One part is either your answer to Step 2 or its opposite. The other part should be the opposite of a perfect square.

$$-37x^2y^2 = -12x^2y^2 - 25x^2y^2$$

Step 4 Rewrite the trinomial as the difference of two squares and then factor.

$$
\begin{aligned}
4x^4 - 37x^2y^2 + 9y^4 &= (4x^4 - 12x^2y^2 + 9y^4) - 25x^2y^2 \\
&= (2x^2 - 3y^2)^2 - 25x^2y^2 \\
&= [(2x^2 - 3y^2) + 5xy][(2x^2 - 3y^2) - 5xy] \\
&= (2x^2 + 5xy - 3y^2)(2x^2 - 5xy - 3y^2)
\end{aligned}
$$

Factor each trinomial.

1. $x^4 + x^2y^2 + y^4$
   $(x^2 + xy + y^2)(x^2 - xy + y^2)$

2. $x^4 + x^2 + 1$
   $(x^2 + x + 1)(x^2 - x + 1)$

3. $9a^4 - 15a^2 + 1$
   $(3a^2 + 3a - 1)(3a^2 - 3a - 1)$

4. $16a^4 - 17a^2 + 1$
   $(4a - 1)(a + 1)(4a + 1)(a - 1)$

5. $4a^4 - 13a^2 + 1$
   $(2a^2 + 3a - 1)(2a^2 - 3a - 1)$

6. $9a^4 + 26a^2b^2 + 25b^4$
   $(3a^2 + 2ab + 5b^2)(3a^2 - 2ab + 5b^2)$

7. $4x^4 - 21x^2y^2 + 9y^4$
   $(2x^2 + 3xy - 3y^2)(2x^2 - 3xy - 3y^2)$

8. $4a^4 - 29a^2c^2 + 25c^4$
   $(2a + 5c)(a - c)(2a - 5c)(a + c)$

 Algebra: Concepts and Applications

NAME _____ DATE _____ PERIOD _____

Enrichment

Student Edition
Pages 445–449

Writing Expressions of Area in Factored Form

Write an expression in factored form for the area A of the
shaded region in each figure below.

1.

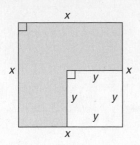

2.

3.

4.

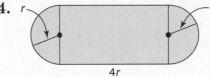

5.

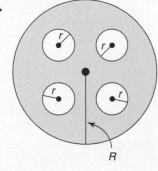

6.

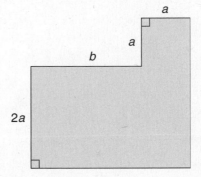

7.

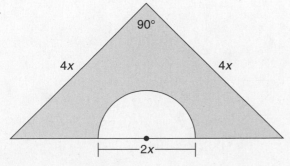

8.

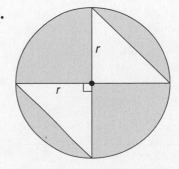

Algebra: Concepts and Applications

Enrichment

Writing Expressions of Area in Factored Form

Write an expression in factored form for the area A of the shaded region in each figure below.

1.
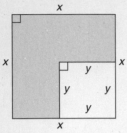
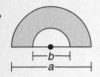

$$A = (x + y)(x - y)$$

2.
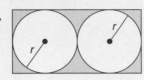

$$A = 2r^2(4 - \pi)$$

3.
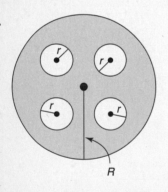

$$A = \frac{\pi}{8}(a + b)(a - b)$$

4.
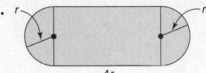

$$A = r^2(8 + \pi)$$

5.
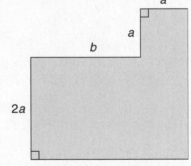

$$A = \pi(R + 2r)(R - 2r)$$

6.

$$A = a(3a + 2b)$$

7.
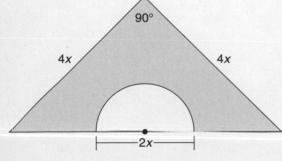

$$A = x^2\left(8 - \frac{\pi}{2}\right)$$

8.
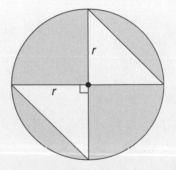

$$A = r^2(\pi - 1)$$

Algebra: Concepts and Applications

11-1

Enrichment

Student Edition
Pages 458–463

Odd Numbers and Parabolas

The solid parabola and the dashed stair-step graph
are related. The parabola intersects the stair steps at
their inside corners.

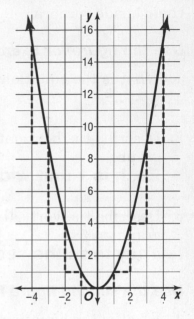

Use the figure for Exercises 1–3.

1. What is the equation of the parabola?

2. Describe the horizontal sections of the stair-step
   graph.

3. Describe the vertical sections of the stair-step
   graph.

Use the second figure for Exercises 4–6.

4. What is the equation of the parabola?

5. Describe the horizontal sections of the stair steps.

6. Describe the vertical sections.

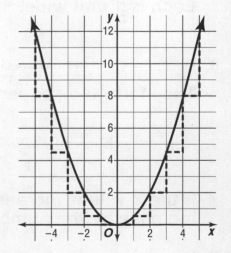

7. How does the graph of $y = \frac{1}{2}x^2$ relate to the

   sequence of numbers $\frac{1}{2}, \frac{3}{2}, \frac{5}{2}, \frac{7}{2}, \cdots$?

8. Complete this conclusion. To graph a parabola
   with the equation $y = ax^2$, start at the vertex.
   Then go over 1 and up a; over 1 and up $3a$;

   _____

   _____

   _____

65

Odd Numbers and Parabolas

The solid parabola and the dashed stair-step graph
are related. The parabola intersects the stair steps at
their inside corners.

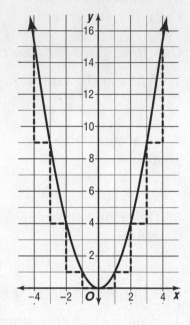

Use the figure for Exercises 1–3.

1. What is the equation of the parabola?
$y = x^2$

2. Describe the horizontal sections of the stair-step
graph.
Each is 1 unit wide.

3. Describe the vertical sections of the stair-step
graph.
They form the sequence 1, 3, 5, 7.

Use the second figure for Exercises 4–6.

4. What is the equation of the parabola?
$y = \frac{1}{2}x^2$

5. Describe the horizontal sections of the stair steps.
Each is 1 unit wide.

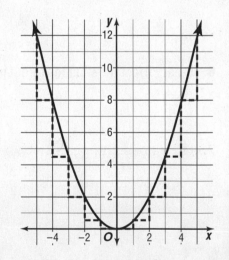

6. Describe the vertical sections.
They form the sequence $\frac{1}{2}, \frac{3}{2}, \frac{5}{2}, \frac{7}{2}, \frac{9}{2}$.

7. How does the graph of $y = \frac{1}{2}x^2$ relate to the
sequence of numbers $\frac{1}{2}, \frac{3}{2}, \frac{5}{2}, \frac{7}{2}, \cdots$?
**If the x-values increase by 1, the y-values
increase by the numbers in the sequence.**

8. Complete this conclusion. To graph a parabola
with the equation $y = ax^2$, start at the vertex.
Then go over 1 and up a; over 1 and up $3a$;

over 1 and up 5a; over 1 and up 7a,

and so on; the coefficients of a are

the odd numbers.

11-2

Enrichment

Student Edition
Pages 464–467

Translating Quadratic Graphs

When a figure is moved to a new position without undergoing any rotation, then the figure is said to have been **translated** to the new position.

The graph of a quadratic equation in the form $y = (x - b)^2 + c$ is a translation of the graph of $y = x^2$.

Start with $y = x^2$.
Slide to the right 4 units.

$$y = (x - 4)^2$$

Then slide up 3 units.

$$y = (x - 4)^2 + 3$$

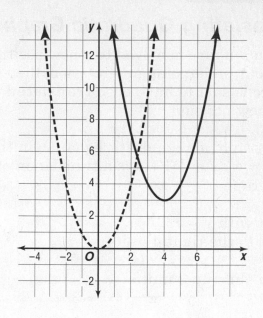

These equations have the form $y = x^2 + c$. Graph each equation.

1. $y = x^2 + 1$

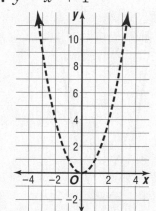

2. $y = x^2 + 2$

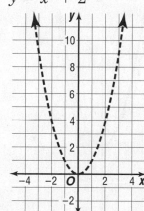

3. $y = x^2 - 2$

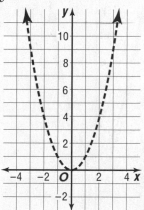

These equations have the form $y = (x - b)^2$. Graph each equation.

4. $y = (x - 1)^2$

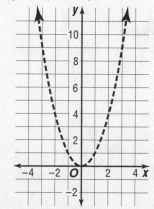

5. $y = (x - 3)^2$

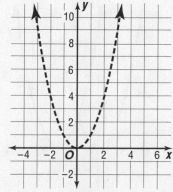

6. $y = (x + 2)^2$

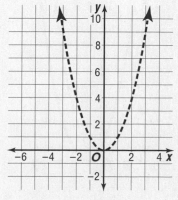

Algebra: Concepts and Applications

11-2

Enrichment

Student Edition
Pages 464–467

Translating Quadratic Graphs

When a figure is moved to a new position without undergoing any rotation, then the figure is said to have been **translated** to the new position.

The graph of a quadratic equation in the form $y = (x - b)^2 + c$ is a translation of the graph of $y = x^2$.

Start with $y = x^2$.
Slide to the right 4 units.
$$y = (x - 4)^2$$
Then slide up 3 units.
$$y = (x - 4)^2 + 3$$

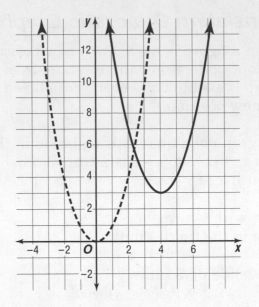

These equations have the form y = x² + c. Graph each equation.

1. $y = x^2 + 1$

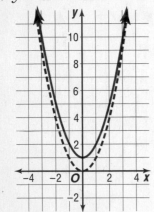

2. $y = x^2 + 2$

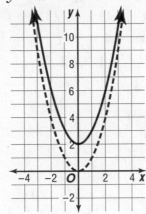

3. $y = x^2 - 2$

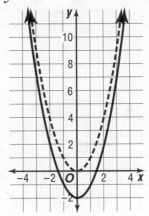

These equations have the form y = (x − b)². Graph each equation.

4. $y = (x - 1)^2$

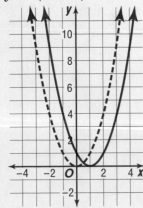

5. $y = (x - 3)^2$

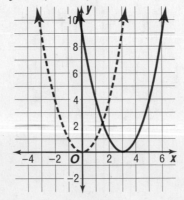

6. $y = (x + 2)^2$

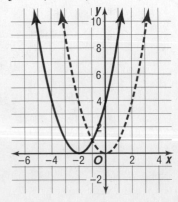

Algebra: Concepts and Applications

Enrichment

Student Edition
Pages 468–473

Polynomial Functions

Suppose a linear equation such as $-3x + y = 4$ is solved for y. Then an equivalent equation, $y = 3x + 4$, is found. Expressed in this way, y is a function of x, or $f(x) = 3x + 4$. Notice that the right side of the equation is a binomial of degree 1.

Higher-degree polynomials in x may also form functions. An example is $f(x) = x^3 + 1$, which is a polynomial function of degree 3. You can graph this function using a table of ordered pairs.

x	y
$-1\frac{1}{2}$	$-2\frac{2}{8}$
-1	0
0	1
1	2
$1\frac{1}{2}$	$4\frac{3}{8}$

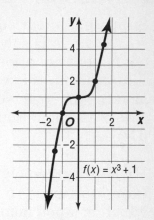

$f(x) = x^3 + 1$

For each of the following polynomial functions, make a table of values for x and y = f(x). Then draw the graph on the grid.

1. $f(x) = 1 - x^2$

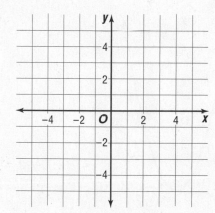

2. $f(x) = x^2 - 5$

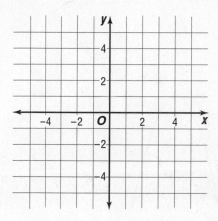

3. $f(x) = x^2 + 4x - 1$

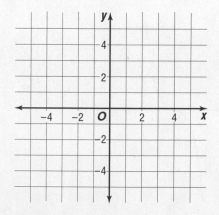

4. $f(x) = x^3$

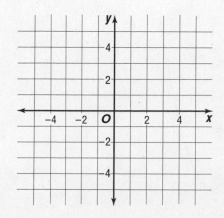

Algebra: Concepts and Applications

11-3 Enrichment

Polynomial Functions

Suppose a linear equation such as
$-3x + y = 4$ is solved for y. Then an
equivalent equation, $y = 3x + 4$, is found.
Expressed in this way, y is a function of x,
or $f(x) = 3x + 4$. Notice that the right
side of the equation is a binomial of
degree 1.

Higher-degree polynomials in x may also
form functions. An example is $f(x) = x^3 + 1$,
which is a polynomial function of degree 3.
You can graph this function using a table
of ordered pairs.

x	y
$-1\frac{1}{2}$	$-2\frac{2}{8}$
-1	0
0	1
1	2
$1\frac{1}{2}$	$4\frac{3}{8}$

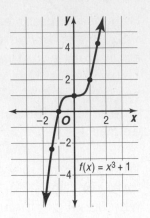

**For each of the following polynomial functions, make a table
of values for x and y = f(x). Then draw the graph on the grid.**

1. $f(x) = 1 - x^2$

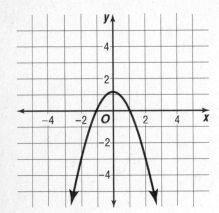

2. $f(x) = x^2 - 5$

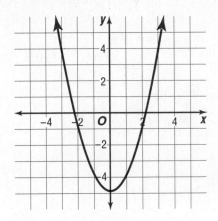

3. $f(x) = x^2 + 4x - 1$

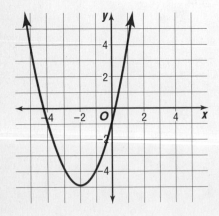

4. $f(x) = x^3$

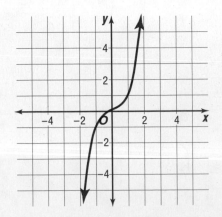

Algebra: Concepts and Applications

Surface Area of Solid Figures

Many solid objects are formed by rectangles and squares. A box is an example.

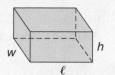

The dimensions of the box shown at the right are represented by letters. The length of the base is ℓ units, its width is w units, and the height of the box is h units.

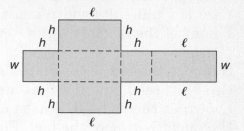

Suppose the box is cut on the seams so that it can be spread out on a flattened surface as shown at the right. The area of this figure is the surface area of the box. Find a formula for the surface area of the box.

There are 6 rectangles in the figure. The surface area is the sum of the areas of the 6 rectangles.

$$S = hw + h\ell + \ell w + h\ell + hw + \ell w$$
$$S = 2\ell w + 2h\ell + 2hw$$

Find the surface area of a box with the given dimensions.

1. $\ell = 14$ cm, $w = 8$ cm, $h = 2$ cm

2. $\ell = 40$ cm, $w = 30$ cm, $h = 25$ cm

3. $\ell = x$ cm, $w = (x - 3)$ cm, $h = (x + 3)$ cm

4. $\ell = (s + 9)$ cm, $w = (s - 9)$ cm, $h = (s + 9)$ cm

5. The surface area of a box is 142 cm². The length of the base is 2 cm longer than its width. The height of the box is 2 cm less than the width of the base. Find the dimensions of the box.

6. Write an expression that represents the surface area of the figure shown at the right. Include the surface area of the base.

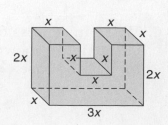

11-4

Enrichment

Student Edition
Pages 474–477

Surface Area of Solid Figures

Many solid objects are formed by rectangles and squares. A box is an example.

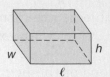

The dimensions of the box shown at the right are represented by letters. The length of the base is ℓ units, its width is w units, and the height of the box is h units.

Suppose the box is cut on the seams so that it can be spread out on a flattened surface as shown at the right. The area of this figure is the surface area of the box. Find a formula for the surface area of the box.

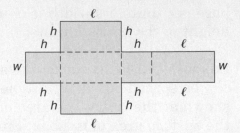

There are 6 rectangles in the figure. The surface area is the sum of the areas of the 6 rectangles.

$$S = hw + h\ell + \ell w + h\ell + hw + \ell w$$
$$S = 2\ell w + 2h\ell + 2hw$$

Find the surface area of a box with the given dimensions.

1. $\ell = 14$ cm, $w = 8$ cm, $h = 2$ cm
   312 cm²

2. $\ell = 40$ cm, $w = 30$ cm, $h = 25$ cm
   5900 cm²

3. $\ell = x$ cm, $w = (x - 3)$ cm,
   $h = (x + 3)$ cm **6(x² − 3) cm²**

4. $\ell = (s + 9)$ cm, $w = (s - 9)$ cm,
   $h = (s + 9)$ cm
   (6s² + 36s − 162) cm²

5. The surface area of a box is 142 cm². The length of the base is 2 cm longer than its width. The height of the box is 2 cm less than the width of the base. Find the dimensions of the box.
   w = 5 cm; ℓ = w + 2 or 7 cm; h = w − 2 or 3 cm

6. Write an expression that represents the surface area of the figure shown at the right. Include the surface area of the base. **22x²**

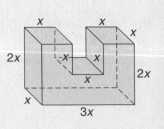

         Algebra: Concepts and Applications

Graphing Circles by Completing Squares

One use for completing the square is to graph circles. The general equation for a circle with center at the origin and radius r is $x^2 + y^2 = r^2$. An equation represents a circle if it can be transformed into the sum of two squares.

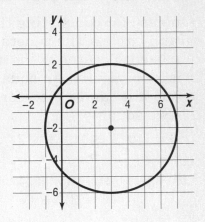

$$x^2 - 6x + y^2 + 4y - 3 = 0$$
$$(x^2 - 6x + 9) + (y^2 + 4y + 4) = 0$$
$$(x^2 - 6x + 9) + (y^2 + 4y + 4) = 3 + 9 + 4$$
$$(x - 3)^2 + (y + 2)^2 = 4^2$$

Notice that the center of the circle is at the point $(3, -2)$.

Transform each equation into the sum of two squares. Then graph the circle represented by the equation. Use the coordinate plane provided at the bottom of the page.

1. $x^2 - 14x + y^2 + 6y + 49 = 0$

2. $x^2 + y^2 - 8y - 9 = 0$

3. $x^2 + 10x + y^2 + 21 = 0$

4. $x^2 + y^2 + 10y + 16 = 0$

5. $x^2 - 30x + y^2 + 209 = 0$

6. $x^2 - 18x + y^2 - 12y + 116 = 0$

7. $x^2 + 30x + y^2 - 4y + 193 = 0$

8. $x^2 + 38x + y^2 - 12y + 393 = 0$

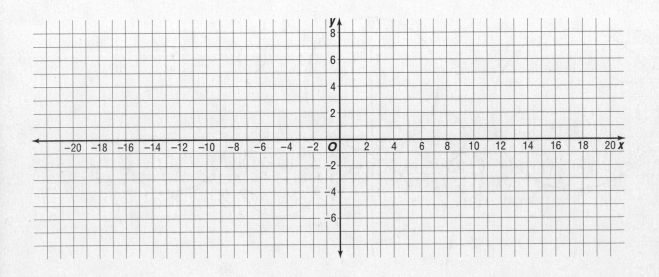

11-5

Enrichment

Student Edition
Pages 478–482

Graphing Circles by Completing Squares

One use for completing the square is to graph circles. The general equation for a circle with center at the origin and radius r is $x^2 + y^2 = r^2$. An equation represents a circle if it can be transformed into the sum of two squares.

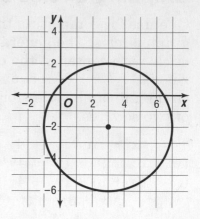

$$x^2 - 6x + y^2 + 4y - 3 = 0$$
$$(x^2 - 6x +) + (y^2 + 4y +) = 0$$
$$(x^2 - 6x + 9) + (y^2 + 4y + 4) = 3 + 9 + 4$$
$$(x - 3)^2 + (y + 2)^2 = 4^2$$

Notice that the center of the circle is at the point $(3, -2)$.

Transform each equation into the sum of two squares. Then graph the circle represented by the equation. Use the coordinate plane provided at the bottom of the page.

1. $x^2 - 14x + y^2 + 6y + 49 = 0$
   $$(x - 7)^2 + (y + 3)^2 = 3^2$$

2. $x^2 + y^2 - 8y - 9 = 0$
   $$x^2 + (y - 4)^2 = 5^2$$

3. $x^2 + 10x + y^2 + 21 = 0$
   $$(x + 5)^2 + y^2 = 2^2$$

4. $x^2 + y^2 + 10y + 16 = 0$
   $$x^2 + (y + 5)^2 = 3^2$$

5. $x^2 - 30x + y^2 + 209 = 0$
   $$(x - 15)^2 + y^2 = 4^2$$

6. $x^2 - 18x + y^2 - 12y + 116 = 0$
   $$(x^2 - 9)^2 + (y - 6)^2 = 1^2$$

7. $x^2 + 30x + y^2 - 4y + 193 = 0$
   $$(x + 15)^2 + (y - 2)^2 = 6^2$$

8. $x^2 + 38x + y^2 - 12y + 393 = 0$
   $$(x + 19)^2 + (y - 6)^2 = 2^2$$

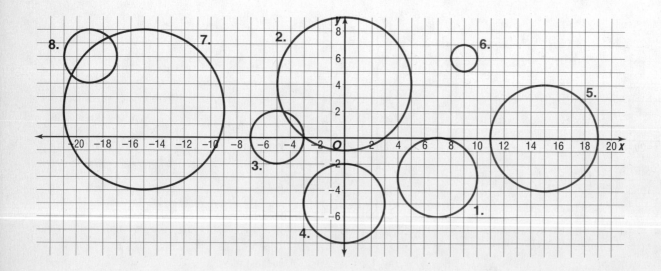

11-6

Enrichment

Golden Rectangles

A **golden rectangle** has the property that its sides satisfy the following proportion.

$$\frac{a + b}{a} = \frac{a}{b}$$

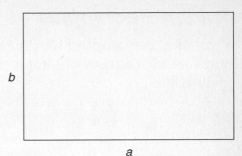

Two quadratic equations can be written from the proportion. These are sometimes called **golden quadratic** equations.

1. In the proportion, let $a = 1$. Use cross-multiplication to write a quadratic equation.

2. Solve the equation in problem 1 for b.

3. In the proportion, let $b = 1$. Write a quadratic equation in a.

4. Solve the equation in problem 3 for a.

5. Explain why $\frac{1}{2}(\sqrt{5} + 1)$ and $\frac{1}{2}(\sqrt{5} - 1)$ are called golden ratios.

Another property of golden rectangles is that a square drawn inside a golden rectangle creates another, smaller golden rectangle.

In the design at the right, opposite vertices of each square have been connected with quarters of circles.

For example, the arc from point B to point C is created by putting the point of a compass at point A. The radius of the arc is the length BA.

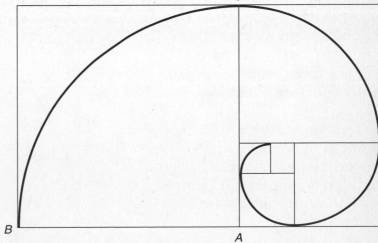

6. On a separate sheet of paper, draw a larger version of the design. Start with a golden rectangle with a long side of 10 inches.

Golden Rectangles

A **golden rectangle** has the property
that its sides satisfy the following
proportion.

$$\frac{a + b}{a} = \frac{a}{b}$$

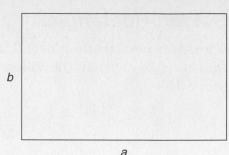

Two quadratic equations can be written from the proportion.
These are sometimes called **golden quadratic** equations.

1. In the proportion, let $a = 1$. Use
   cross-multiplication to write a
   quadratic equation.
   $b^2 + b - 1 = 0$

2. Solve the equation in problem 1
   for b.

   $b = \dfrac{-1 + \sqrt{5}}{2}$

3. In the proportion, let $b = 1$. Write a
   quadratic equation in a.
   $a^2 - a - 1 = 0$

4. Solve the equation in problem 3
   for a.
   $a = \dfrac{1 + \sqrt{5}}{2}$

5. Explain why $\frac{1}{2}(\sqrt{5} + 1)$ and $\frac{1}{2}(\sqrt{5} - 1)$ are called golden ratios.

   **They are the ratios of the sides in a golden
   rectangle. The first is the ratio of the long
   side to the short side; the second is short
   side: long side.**

Another property of golden rectangles is that a square drawn
inside a golden rectangle creates another, smaller golden
rectangle.

In the design at the right,
opposite vertices of each
square have been connected
with quarters of circles.

For example, the arc from
point B to point C is
created by putting the
point of a compass at point
A. The radius of the arc is
the length BA.

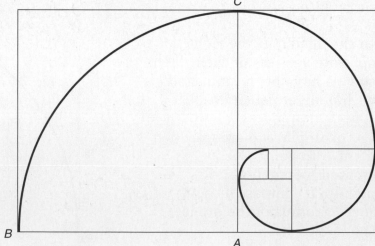

6. On a separate sheet of paper, draw a larger version of the
   design. Start with a golden rectangle with a long side of
   10 inches.

   The short side should be about $6\frac{3}{16}$ inches.

11-7

Enrichment

Applications of Geometric Sequence

Populations often grow according to a geometric sequence. If the population of a country grows at the rate of 2% per year, then the common ratio, r, is 1.02. To find the population of a city of 100,000 after 5 years of 2% growth, use the formula ar^{n-1}, where r is the common ratio and n is the number of years.

$$ar^{n-1} = 100{,}000 \times 1.02^{5-1} \qquad a = 100{,}000;\ r = 1.02;\ n = 5$$

$$= 100{,}000 \times 1.02^4$$

$$\approx 108{,}243$$

After a few years, a small change in the annual growth rate can cause enormous differences in the population.

Assume that the nation of Grogro had a population of one million in 1990. Using a calculator, find the population of the country in the years 2000, 2050, and 2100 at growth rates of 1%, 3%, and 5% per year. Record your results in the table below.

	Growth Rate	Population of Grogro		
		Year		
		2000	2050	2100
1.	1%			
2.	3%			
3.	5%			

Suppose we want to find the *total* distance a bouncing ball has moved. We need a formula for the *sum* of the terms of a geometric sequence. This is called a **geometric series**.

$$S_n = \frac{a - ar^n}{1 - r} \qquad \begin{array}{l} a = \textit{first term} \\ r = \textit{common ratio } (r \neq 1) \\ n = \textit{number of terms} \end{array}$$

Use the formula above to find each sum. Then check your answer by adding.

4. $5 + 10 + 20 + 40 + 80$

5. $80 + 240 + 720 + 2160 + 6480$

Applications of Geometric Sequence

Populations often grow according to a geometric sequence. If the population of a country grows at the rate of 2% per year, then the common ratio, r, is 1.02. To find the population of a city of 100,000 after 5 years of 2% growth, use the formula ar^{n-1}, where r is the common ratio and n is the number of years.

$ar^{n-1} = 100,000 \times 1.02^{5-1}$ $a = 100,000; r = 1.02; n = 5$

$= 100,000 \times 1.02^4$

$\approx 108,243$

After a few years, a small change in the annual growth rate can cause enormous differences in the population.

Assume that the nation of Grogro had a population of one million in 1990. Using a calculator, find the population of the country in the years 2000, 2050, and 2100 at growth rates of 1%, 3%, and 5% per year. Record your results in the table below.

	Growth Rate	Population of Grogro		
		Year		
		2000	2050	2100
1.	1%	1,093,685	1,798,709	2,958,215
2.	3%	1,304,773	5,720,003	25,075,956
3.	5%	1,551,328	17,789,701	204,001,612

Suppose we want to find the *total* distance a bouncing ball has moved. We need a formula for the *sum* of the terms of a geometric sequence. This is called a **geometric series**.

$S_n = \dfrac{a - ar^n}{1 - r}$ $a = first\ term$
$r = common\ ratio\ (r \neq 1)$
$n = number\ of\ terms$

Use the formula above to find each sum. Then check your answer by adding.

4. $5 + 10 + 20 + 40 + 80$ **155**

5. $80 + 240 + 720 + 2160 + 6480$
   9680

Enrichment

Intersection and Union

The **intersection** of two sets is the set of elements that are
in both of the sets. The intersection of sets A and B is written
A ∩ B. The **union** of two sets is the set of elements in either A,
or in B, or in both. The union is written A ∪ B.

In the drawings below, suppose A is the set of points inside
the circle and B is the set of points inside the square. Then,
the shaded areas show the intersection and union.

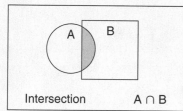 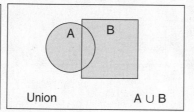

Intersection   A ∩ B   Union   A ∪ B

Write A ∩ B and A ∪ B for each of the following.

1. A = {p, q, r, s, t}   B = {q, r, s} _____

2. A = {the integers between 2 and 7} B = {0, 3, 8} _____

3. A = {the states whose names start with K}
   B = {the states whose capital is Honolulu or Topeka} _____

4. A = {the positive integer factors of 24}
   B = {the counting numbers less than 10} _____

**Suppose A = {numbers x such that x < 3}, B = {numbers x
such that x ≥ − 1}, and C = {numbers x such that x ≤ 1.5}.
Graph each of the following.**

5. A ∩ B

6. A ∪ B

7. B ∪ C

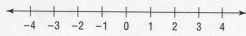

8. B ∩ C

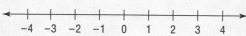

9. (A ∩ C) ∩ B

10. A ∩ (B ∪ C)

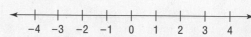

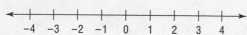 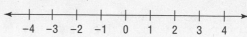

Algebra: Concepts and Applications

Enrichment

Intersection and Union

The **intersection** of two sets is the set of elements that are
in both of the sets. The intersection of sets A and B is written
A ∩ B. The **union** of two sets is the set of elements in either A,
or in B, or in both. The union is written A ∪ B.

In the drawings below, suppose A is the set of points inside
the circle and B is the set of points inside the square. Then,
the shaded areas show the intersection and union.

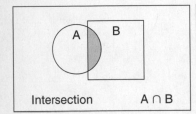
Intersection   A ∩ B

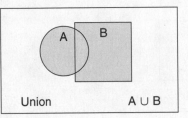
Union   A ∪ B

Write A ∩ B and A ∪ B for each of the following.

1. A = {p, q, r, s, t}   B = {q, r, s}   **A ∩ B = {q, r, s} A ∪ B = {p, q, r, s, t}**

2. A = {the integers between 2 and 7} B = {0, 3, 8}   **A ∩ B = {3}**
   A ∪ B = {0, 3, 4, 5, 6, 8}

3. A = {the states whose names start with K}   **A ∩ B = {Kansas}**
   B = {the states whose capital is Honolulu or Topeka}   **A ∪ B = {Hawaii, Kansas, Kentucky}**

4. A = {the positive integer factors of 24}   **A ∩ B = {1, 2, 3, 4, 6, 8}**
   B = {the counting numbers less than 10}   **A ∪ B = {1, 2, 3, 4, 5, 6, 7, 8, 9, 12, 24}**

**Suppose A = {numbers x such that x < 3}, B = {numbers x
such that x ≥ − 1}, and C = {numbers x such that x ≤ 1.5}.
Graph each of the following.**

5. A ∩ B

6. A ∪ B

7. B ∪ C

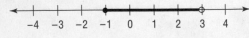

8. B ∩ C

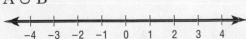

9. (A ∩ C) ∩ B

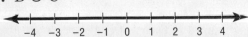

10. A ∩ (B ∪ C)

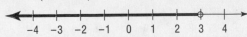

Enrichment

Consecutive Integers and Inequalities

Consecutive integers follow one after another. For example, 4, 5, 6, and 7 are consecutive integers, as are $-8, -7, -6$. Each number to the right in the series is one greater than the one that comes before it. If $x =$ the first consecutive integer, then $x + 1 =$ the second consecutive integer, $x + 2 =$ the third consecutive integer, $x + 3 =$ the fourth consecutive integer, and so on.

Example: Find three consecutive positive integers whose sum is less than 12.

$$\underbrace{x}_{\substack{\text{first} \\ \text{integer}}} + \underbrace{x + 1}_{\substack{\text{second} \\ \text{integer}}} + \underbrace{x + 2}_{\substack{\text{third} \\ \text{integer}}} < 12 \qquad \text{\textit{Simplify the expression by}}$$
$$3x + 3 < 12 \qquad \text{\textit{combining like terms.}}$$

$$3x + 3 - 3 < 12 - 3 \qquad \text{\textit{Subtract 3 from each side.}}$$

$$3x < 9$$

$$\frac{3x}{3} < \frac{9}{3} \qquad \text{\textit{Divide each side by 3.}}$$

$$x < 3 \qquad \text{So } x \text{ could equal 1 or 2.}$$

If $x = 1$, then $x + 1 = 2$, $x + 2 = 3$, and {1, 2, 3} is one solution.

If $x = 2$, then $x + 1 = 3$, $x + 2 = 4$, and {2, 3, 4} is another solution.

Each of the two solutions must be considered in the answer. The solution set is {1, 2, 3; 2, 3, 4}.

Solve. Show all possible solutions.

1. Find three consecutive positive integers whose sum is less than 15.

2. Find two consecutive positive even integers whose sum is less than 10.

3. Find three consecutive positive integers such that the second plus four times the first is less than 21.

4. Find three consecutive positive even integers such that the third plus twice the second is less than 26.

Consecutive Integers and Inequalities

Consecutive integers follow one after another. For example, 4, 5, 6, and 7 are consecutive integers, as are $-8, -7, -6$. Each number to the right in the series is one greater than the one that comes before it. If $x =$ the first consecutive integer, then $x + 1 =$ the second consecutive integer, $x + 2 =$ the third consecutive integer, $x + 3 =$ the fourth consecutive integer, and so on.

Example: Find three consecutive positive integers whose sum is less than 12.

$$
\underbrace{x}_{\substack{\text{first} \\ \text{integer}}} + \underbrace{x + 1}_{\substack{\text{second} \\ \text{integer}}} + \underbrace{x + 2}_{\substack{\text{third} \\ \text{integer}}} < 12 \qquad \textit{Simplify the expression by}
$$

$$
3x + 3 < 12 \qquad \textit{combining like terms.}
$$

$$
3x + 3 - 3 < 12 - 3 \qquad \textit{Subtract 3 from each side.}
$$

$$
3x < 9
$$

$$
\frac{3x}{3} < \frac{9}{3} \qquad \textit{Divide each side by 3.}
$$

$$
x < 3 \qquad \text{So } x \text{ could equal 1 or 2.}
$$

If $x = 1$, then $x + 1 = 2$, $x + 2 = 3$, and $\{1, 2, 3\}$ is one solution.

If $x = 2$, then $x + 1 = 3$, $x + 2 = 4$, and $\{2, 3, 4\}$ is another solution.

Each of the two solutions must be considered in the answer. The solution set is $\{1, 2, 3; 2, 3, 4\}$.

Solve. Show all possible solutions.

1. Find three consecutive positive integers whose sum is less than 15.
{1, 2, 3; 2, 3, 4; 3, 4, 5}

2. Find two consecutive positive even integers whose sum is less than 10.
{2, 4}

3. Find three consecutive positive integers such that the second plus four times the first is less than 21.
{1, 2, 3; 2, 3, 4; 3, 4, 5}

4. Find three consecutive positive even integers such that the third plus twice the second is less than 26.
{2, 4, 6; 4, 6, 8}

Some Properties of Inequalities

The two expressions on either side of an inequality symbol are sometimes called the *first* and *second* members of the inequality.

If the inequality symbols of two inequalities point in the same direction, the inequalities have the same sense. For example, $a < b$ and $c < d$ have the same sense; $a < b$ and $c > d$ have opposite senses.

In the problems on this page, you will explore some properties of inequalities.

Three of the four statements below are true for all numbers a and b (or a, b, c, and d). Write each statement in algebraic form. If the statement is true for all numbers, prove it. If it is not true, give an example to show that it is false.

1. Given an inequality, a new and equivalent inequality can be created by interchanging the members and reversing the sense.

2. Given an inequality, a new and equivalent inequality can be created by changing the signs of both terms and reversing the sense.

3. Given two inequalities with the same sense, the sum of the corresponding members are members of an equivalent inequality with the same sense.

4. Given two inequalities with the same sense, the difference of the corresponding members are members of an equivalent inequality with the same sense.

Enrichment

Some Properties of Inequalities

The two expressions on either side of an inequality symbol are sometimes called the *first* and *second* members of the inequality.

If the inequality symbols of two inequalities point in the same direction, the inequalities have the same sense. For example, $a < b$ and $c < d$ have the same sense; $a < b$ and $c > d$ have opposite senses.

In the problems on this page, you will explore some properties of inequalities.

Three of the four statements below are true for all numbers a and b (or a, b, c, and d). Write each statement in algebraic form. If the statement is true for all numbers, prove it. If it is not true, give an example to show that it is false.

1. Given an inequality, a new and equivalent inequality can be created by interchanging the members and reversing the sense.
    If $a > b$, then $b < a$.
    $a > b$, $a - b > 0$, $-b > -a$, $(-1)(-b) < (-1)(-a)$, $b < a$

2. Given an inequality, a new and equivalent inequality can be created by changing the signs of both terms and reversing the sense.
    If $a > b$, then $-a < -b$.
    $a > b$, $a - b > 0$, $-b > -a$, $-a < -b$

3. Given two inequalities with the same sense, the sum of the corresponding members are members of an equivalent inequality with the same sense.
    If $a > b$ and $c > d$, then $a + c > b + d$.
    $a > b$ and $c > d$, so $(a - b)$ and $(c - d)$ are positive numbers, so the sum $(a - b) + (c - d)$ is also positive.
    $a - b + c - d > 0$, so $a + c > b + d$.

4. Given two inequalities with the same sense, the difference of the corresponding members are members of an equivalent inequality with the same sense.
    If $a > b$ and $c > d$, then $a - c > b - d$. The statement is false. $5 > 4$ and $3 > 2$, but $5 - 3 \not> 4 - 2$.

Algebra: Concepts and Applications

12-4

Enrichment

Consecutive Integer Problems

Many types of problems and puzzles involve the idea of consecutive integers. Here is an example.

Find four consecutive odd integers whose sum is −80.

An odd integer can be written as $2n + 1$, where n is any of the numbers 0, 1, 2, 3, and so on. Then, the equation for the problem is as follows.

$$(2n + 1) + (2n + 3) + (2n + 5) + (2n + 7) = -80$$

Solve these problems. Write an equation or inequality for each.

1. Complete the solution to the problem in the example.

2. Find three consecutive even integers whose sum is 132.

3. Find the two least consecutive integers whose sum is greater than 20.

4. Find the two greatest consecutive integers whose sum is less than 100.

5. The lesser of two consecutive even integers is 10 more than one-half the greater. Find the integers.

6. The greater of two consecutive even integers is 6 less than three times the lesser. Find the integers.

7. Find four consecutive integers such that twice the sum of the two greater integers exceeds three times the first by 91.

8. Find all sets of four consecutive positive integers such that the greatest integer in the set is greater than twice the least integer in the set.

Consecutive Integer Problems

Many types of problems and puzzles involve the idea of consecutive integers. Here is an example.

Find four consecutive odd integers whose sum is −80.

An odd integer can be written as $2n + 1$, where n is any of the numbers 0, 1, 2, 3, and so on. Then, the equation for the problem is as follows.

$$(2n + 1) + (2n + 3) + (2n + 5) + (2n + 7) = -80$$

Solve these problems. Write an equation or inequality for each.

1. Complete the solution to the problem in the example.
   $n = -12$; The integers are −23, −21, −19, −17.

2. Find three consecutive even integers whose sum is 132.
   $2n + (2n + 2) + (2n + 4) = 132$; $n = 21$; Integers are 42, 44, 46.

3. Find the two least consecutive integers whose sum is greater than 20.
   $n + (n + 1) > 20$; $n > 9.5$; Integers are 10 and 11.

4. Find the two greatest consecutive integers whose sum is less than 100.
   $n + (n + 1) < 100$; $n < 49.5$; Integers are 49 and 50.

5. The lesser of two consecutive even integers is 10 more than one-half the greater. Find the integers.
   $2n = 10 + \frac{1}{2}(2n + 2$; $n = 11$; Integers are 22 and 24.

6. The greater of two consecutive even integers is 6 less than three times the lesser. Find the integers.
   $2n + 2 = 3(2n) - 6$; $n = 2$; Integers are 4 and 6.

7. Find four consecutive integers such that twice the sum of the two greater integers exceeds three times the first by 91.
   $2[(n + 2) + (n + 3)] = 3n + 91$; $n = 81$; Integers are 81, 82, 83, 84.

8. Find all sets of four consecutive positive integers such that the greatest integer in the set is greater than twice the least integer in the set.
   $n + 3 > 2n$; $n < 3$; The two sets are {1, 2, 3, 4} and {2, 3, 4, 5}.

Enrichment

Precision of Measurement

The precision of a measurement depends both on your accuracy in measuring and the number of divisions on the ruler you use. Suppose you measured a length of wood to the nearest one-eighth of an inch and got a length of $6\frac{5}{8}$ in.

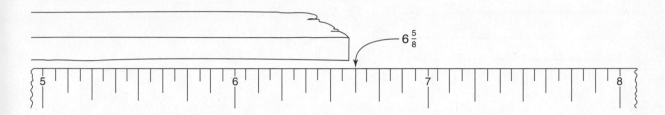

The drawing shows that the actual measurement lies somewhere between $6\frac{9}{16}$ in. and $6\frac{11}{16}$ in. This measurement can be written using the symbol $\pm$, which is read "plus or minus." It can also be written as a compound inequality.

$$6\frac{5}{8} \pm \frac{1}{16} \text{ in.} \qquad\qquad 6\frac{9}{16} \text{ in.} \le m \le 6\frac{11}{16} \text{ in.}$$

In this example, $\frac{1}{16}$ in. is the absolute error. The absolute error is one-half the smallest unit used in a measurement.

Write each measurement as a compound inequality. Use the variable m.

1. $3\frac{1}{2} \pm \frac{1}{4}$ in.

2. 9.78 ± 0.005 cm

3. 2.4 ± 0.05 g

4. $28 \pm \frac{1}{2}$ ft

5. 15 ± 0.5 cm

6. $\frac{11}{16} \pm \frac{1}{64}$ in.

For each measurement, give the smallest unit used and the absolute error.

7. 12.5 cm $\le m \le 13.5$ cm

8. $12\frac{1}{8}$ in. $\le m \le 12\frac{3}{8}$ in.

9. $56\frac{1}{2}$ in. $\le m \le 57\frac{1}{2}$ in.

10. 23.05 mm $\le m \le 23.15$ mm

NAME _____ DATE _____ PERIOD _____

Enrichment

Student Edition
Pages 524–529

Precision of Measurement

The precision of a measurement depends both on your accuracy in measuring and the number of divisions on the ruler you use. Suppose you measured a length of wood to the nearest one-eighth of an inch and got a length of $6\frac{5}{8}$ in.

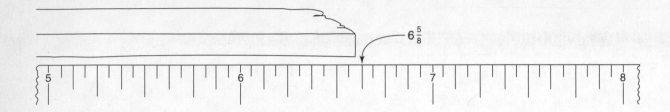

The drawing shows that the actual measurement lies somewhere between $6\frac{9}{16}$ in. and $6\frac{11}{16}$ in. This measurement can be written using the symbol $\pm$, which is read "plus or minus." It can also be written as a compound inequality.

$$6\frac{5}{8} \pm \frac{1}{16} \text{ in.} \qquad\qquad 6\frac{9}{16} \text{ in.} \le m \le 6\frac{11}{16} \text{ in.}$$

In this example, $\frac{1}{16}$ in. is the absolute error. The absolute error is one-half the smallest unit used in a measurement.

Write each measurement as a compound inequality. Use the variable m.

1. $3\frac{1}{2} \pm \frac{1}{4}$ in.

   $3\frac{1}{4}$ **in.** $\le m \le 3\frac{3}{4}$ **in.**

2. 9.78 ± 0.005 cm

   9.775 cm $\le m \le$ **9.785 cm**

3. 2.4 ± 0.05 g

   2.35 g $\le m \le$ **2.45 g**

4. $28 \pm \frac{1}{2}$ ft

   $27\frac{1}{2}$ **ft** $\le m \le 28\frac{1}{2}$ **ft**

5. 15 ± 0.5 cm

   14.5 cm $\le m \le$ **15.5 cm**

6. $\frac{11}{16} \pm \frac{1}{64}$ in.

   $\frac{43}{64}$ **in.** $\le m \le \frac{45}{64}$ **in.**

For each measurement, give the smallest unit used and the absolute error.

7. 12.5 cm $\le m \le 13.5$ cm

   1 cm, 0.5 cm

8. $12\frac{1}{8}$ in. $\le m \le 12\frac{3}{8}$ in.

   $\frac{1}{4}$ **in.,** $\frac{1}{8}$ **in.**

9. $56\frac{1}{2}$ in. $\le m \le 57\frac{1}{2}$ in.

   1 in., $\frac{1}{2}$ **in.**

10. 23.05 mm $\le m \le 23.15$ mm

    0.1 mm, 0.05 mm

Algebra: Concepts and Applications

NAME _____ DATE _____ PERIOD _____

Enrichment

Student Edition
Pages 530–534

Absolute Value Functions

Some types of functions that occur frequently have special
names. Absolute value functions are an example.

Example: Graph $y = |x + 2|$.

x	y
−4	2
−3	1
−2	0
−1	1
0	2
1	3
2	4

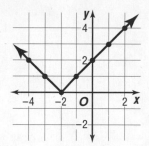

Complete the table for each equation. Then, draw the graph.

1. $y = |x|$

x	y
−3	
−2	
−1	
0	
1	
2	
3	

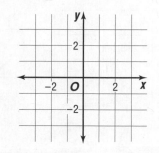

2. $y = |x| - 2$

x	y
−3	
−2	
−1	
0	
1	
2	
3	

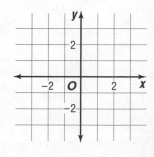

3. $y = |x - 1|$

x	y
−2	
−1	
0	
1	
2	
3	
4	

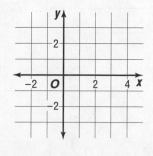

4. $y = |2 - x|$

x	y
−2	
−1	
0	
1	
2	
3	
4	

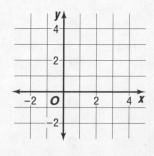

     Algebra: Concepts and Applications

12-6

Enrichment

Student Edition
Pages 530–534

Absolute Value Functions

Some types of functions that occur frequently have special
names. Absolute value functions are an example.

Example: Graph $y = |x + 2|$.

x	y
−4	2
−3	1
−2	0
−1	1
0	2
1	3
2	4

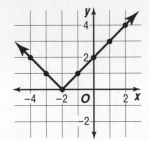

Complete the table for each equation. Then, draw the graph.

1. $y = |x|$

x	y
−3	3
−2	2
−1	1
0	0
1	1
2	2
3	3

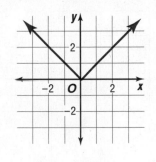

2. $y = |x| - 2$

x	y
−3	1
−2	0
−1	−1
0	−2
1	−1
2	0
3	1

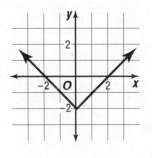

3. $y = |x - 1|$

x	y
−2	3
−1	2
0	1
1	0
2	1
3	2
4	3

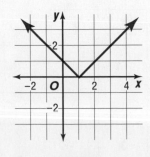

4. $y = |2 - x|$

x	y
−2	4
−1	3
0	2
1	1
2	0
3	1
4	2

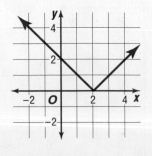

Algebra: Concepts and Applications

12-7

Enrichment

Student Edition
Pages 535–539

Inequalities with Triangles

Recall that a line segment can be named by the letters of its endpoints. Line segment AB (written as "$\overline{AB}$") has points A and B for endpoints. The *length* of AB is written without the bar as AB.

$$AB < BC \qquad\qquad \angle A < \angle B$$

The statement on the left above shows that $\overline{AB}$ is shorter than $\overline{BC}$. The statement on the right above shows that the measure of angle A is less than that of angle B.

These three inequalities are true for any triangle ABC, no matter how long the sides are.

a. $AB + BC > AC$
b. If $AB > AC$, then $\angle C > \angle B$.
c. If $\angle C > \angle B$, then $AB > AC$.

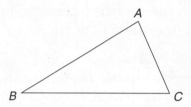

Use the three triangle inequalities for these problems.

1. List the sides of triangle DEF in order of increasing length.

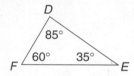

2. In the figure below, which line segment is the shortest?

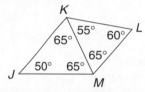

3. Explain why the lengths 5 cm, 10 cm, and 20 cm could not be used to make a triangle.

4. Two sides of a triangle measure 3 in. and 7 in. Between which two values must the third side be?

5. In triangle XYZ, $XY = 15$, $YZ = 12$, and $XZ = 9$. Which is the greatest angle? Which is the least?

6. List the angles $\angle A$, $\angle C$, $\angle ABC$, and $\angle ABD$, in order of increasing size.

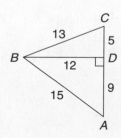

Algebra: Concepts and Applications

Inequalities with Triangles

Recall that a line segment can be named by the letters of its endpoints. Line segment AB (written as "$\overline{AB}$") has points A and B for endpoints. The *length* of AB is written without the bar as AB.

$$AB < BC \qquad\qquad\qquad \angle A < \angle B$$

The statement on the left above shows that $\overline{AB}$ is shorter than $\overline{BC}$. The statement on the right above shows that the measure of angle A is less than that of angle B.

These three inequalities are true for any triangle ABC, no matter how long the sides are.

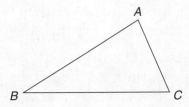

a. $AB + BC > AC$
b. If $AB > AC$, then $\angle C > \angle B$.
c. If $\angle C > \angle B$, then $AB > AC$.

Use the three triangle inequalities for these problems.

1. List the sides of triangle DEF in order of increasing length.
   $\overline{DF}, \overline{DE}, \overline{EF}$

2. In the figure below, which line segment is the shortest?
   $\overline{LM}$

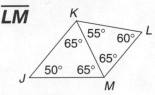

3. Explain why the lengths 5 cm, 10 cm, and 20 cm could not be used to make a triangle. **5 + 10 is not greater than 20.**

4. Two sides of a triangle measure 3 in. and 7 in. Between which two values must the third side be? **4 in. and 10 in.**

5. In triangle XYZ, $XY = 15$, $YZ = 12$, and $XZ = 9$. Which is the greatest angle? Which is the least?
   $\angle Z$; $\angle Y$

6. List the angles $\angle A$, $\angle C$, $\angle ABC$, and $\angle ABD$, in order of increasing size.
   $\angle ABD$, $\angle A$, $\angle ABC$, $\angle C$

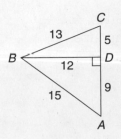

Graphing a Trip

The formula $d = rt$ is used to solve many types
of problems. If you graph an equation such as
$d = 50t$, the graph is a model for a car going at
50 mi/h. The time the car travels is t; the distance
in miles the car covers is d. The slope of the line is
the speed.

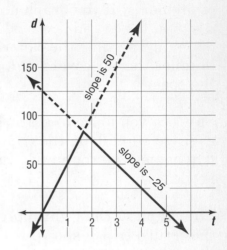

Suppose you drive to a nearby town and return. You
average 50 mi/h on the trip out but only 25 mi/h on the
trip home. The round trip takes 5 hours. How far away
is the town?

The graph at the right represents your trip. Notice that
the return trip is shown with a negative slope because
you are driving in the opposite direction.

Solve each problem.

1. Estimate the answer to the problem in the above
   example. About how far away is the town?

2. Graph this trip and solve the problem. An airplane
   has enough fuel for 3 hours of safe flying. On the
   trip out the pilot averages 200 mi/h flying against
   a headwind. On the trip back, the pilot averages
   250 mi/h. How long a trip out can the pilot make?

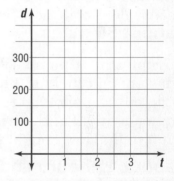

3. Graph this trip and solve the problem.
   You drive to a town 100 miles away.
   On the trip out you average 25 mi/h.
   On the trip back you average 50 mi/h.
   How many hours do you spend
   driving?

4. Graph this trip and solve the problem.
   You drive at an average speed of 50
   mi/h to a discount shopping plaza,
   spend 2 hours shopping, and then
   return at an average speed of 25 mi/h.
   The entire trip takes 8 hours. How far
   away is the shopping plaza?

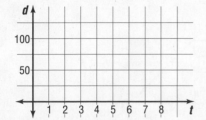

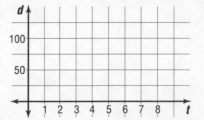

Graphing a Trip

The formula $d = rt$ is used to solve many types
of problems. If you graph an equation such as
$d = 50t$, the graph is a model for a car going at
50 mi/h. The time the car travels is t; the distance
in miles the car covers is d. The slope of the line is
the speed.

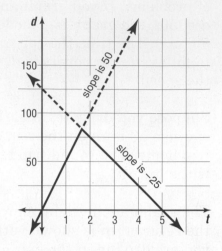

Suppose you drive to a nearby town and return. You
average 50 mi/h on the trip out but only 25 mi/h on the
trip home. The round trip takes 5 hours. How far away
is the town?

The graph at the right represents your trip. Notice that
the return trip is shown with a negative slope because
you are driving in the opposite direction.

Solve each problem.

1. Estimate the answer to the problem in the above
   example. About how far away is the town?
   about 80 miles

2. Graph this trip and solve the problem. An airplane
   has enough fuel for 3 hours of safe flying. On the
   trip out the pilot averages 200 mi/h flying against
   a headwind. On the trip back, the pilot averages
   250 mi/h. How long a trip out can the pilot make?

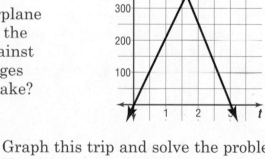

   about $1\frac{2}{3}$ hours and 330 miles

3. Graph this trip and solve the problem.
   You drive to a town 100 miles away.
   On the trip out you average 25 mi/h.
   On the trip back you average 50 mi/h.
   How many hours do you spend
   driving?
   6 hours

4. Graph this trip and solve the problem.
   You drive at an average speed of 50
   mi/h to a discount shopping plaza,
   spend 2 hours shopping, and then
   return at an average speed of 25 mi/h.
   The entire trip takes 8 hours. How far
   away is the shopping plaza? **100 miles**

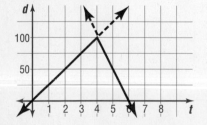

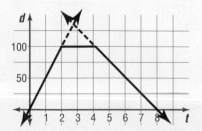

13-2

Enrichment

Convergence, Divergence, and Limits

Imagine that a runner runs a mile from point A to point B. But, this is not an ordinary race! In the first minute, he runs one-half mile, reaching point C. In the next minute, he covers one-half the remaining distance, or $\frac{1}{4}$ mile, reaching point D. In the next minute he covers one-half the remaining distance, or $\frac{1}{8}$ mile, reaching point E.

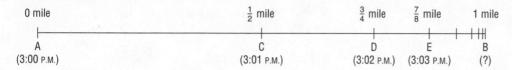

In this strange race, the runner approaches closer and closer to point B, but never gets there. However close he is to B, there is still some distance remaining, and in the next minute he can cover only half of that distance.

This race can be modeled by the infinite sequence

$$\frac{1}{2}, \frac{3}{4}, \frac{7}{8}, \frac{15}{16}, \cdots .$$

The terms of the sequence get closer and closer to 1. An infinite sequence that gets arbitrarily close to some number is said to **converge** to that number. The number is the limit of the sequence.

Not all infinite sequences converge. Those that do not are called **divergent.**

Write C if the sequence converges and D if it diverges. If the sequence converges, make a reasonable guess for its limit.

1. 2, 4, 6, 8, 10, $\cdots$

2. 0, 3, 0, 3, 0, 3, $\cdots$

3. 1, $\frac{1}{2}, \frac{1}{3}, \frac{1}{4}, \frac{1}{5},$ $\cdots$

4. 0.9, 0.99, 0.999, 0.9999, $\cdots$

5. $-5, 5, -5, 5, -5, 5,$ $\cdots$

6. 0.1, 0.2, 0.3, 0.4, $\cdots$

7. $2\frac{1}{4}, 2\frac{3}{4}, 2\frac{7}{8}, 2\frac{15}{16},$ $\cdots$

8. 6, $5\frac{1}{2}, 5\frac{1}{3}, 5\frac{1}{4}, 5\frac{1}{5},$ $\cdots$

9. 1, 4, 9, 16, 25, $\cdots$

10. 1, $-\frac{1}{2}, \frac{1}{3}, -\frac{1}{4}, \frac{1}{5}, -\frac{1}{6},$ $\cdots$

11. Create one convergent sequence and one divergent sequence. Give the limit for your convergent sequence.

Algebra: Concepts and Applications

Convergence, Divergence, and Limits

Imagine that a runner runs a mile from point A to point B. But, this is not an ordinary race! In the first minute, he runs one-half mile, reaching point C. In the next minute, he covers one-half the remaining distance, or $\frac{1}{4}$ mile, reaching point D. In the next minute he covers one-half the remaining distance, or $\frac{1}{8}$ mile, reaching point E.

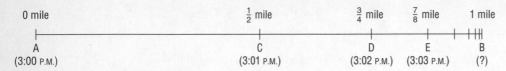

| 0 mile | | | $\frac{1}{2}$ mile | $\frac{3}{4}$ mile | $\frac{7}{8}$ mile | 1 mile |

A
(3:00 P.M.)   C
(3:01 P.M.)   D
(3:02 P.M.)   E
(3:03 P.M.)   B
(?)

In this strange race, the runner approaches closer and closer to point B, but never gets there. However close he is to B, there is still some distance remaining, and in the next minute he can cover only half of that distance.

This race can be modeled by the infinite sequence
$\frac{1}{2}, \frac{3}{4}, \frac{7}{8}, \frac{15}{16}, \cdots$.

The terms of the sequence get closer and closer to 1. An infinite sequence that gets arbitrarily close to some number is said to **converge** to that number. The number is the limit of the sequence.

Not all infinite sequences converge. Those that do not are called **divergent**.

Write C if the sequence converges and D if it diverges. If the sequence converges, make a reasonable guess for its limit.

1. 2, 4, 6, 8, 10, $\cdots$ __D__

2. 0, 3, 0, 3, 0, 3, $\cdots$ __D__

3. 1, $\frac{1}{2}, \frac{1}{3}, \frac{1}{4}, \frac{1}{5}, \cdots$ __C, 0__

4. 0.9, 0.99, 0.999, 0.9999, $\cdots$ __C, 1__

5. $-5, 5, -5, 5, -5, 5, \cdots$ __D__

6. 0.1, 0.2, 0.3, 0.4, $\cdots$ __D__

7. $2\frac{1}{4}, 2\frac{3}{4}, 2\frac{7}{8}, 2\frac{15}{16}, \cdots$ __C, 3__

8. 6, $5\frac{1}{2}, 5\frac{1}{3}, 5\frac{1}{4}, 5\frac{1}{5}, \cdots$ __C, 5__

9. 1, 4, 9, 16, 25, $\cdots$ __D__

10. 1, $-\frac{1}{2}, \frac{1}{3}, -\frac{1}{4}, \frac{1}{5}, -\frac{1}{6}, \cdots$ __C, 0__

11. Create one convergent sequence and one divergent sequence. Give the limit for your convergent sequence.
See students' work.

13-3

Enrichment

Investments

The graph below represents two different investments. Line A represents an initial investment of $30,000 at a bank paying passbook-savings interest. Line B represents an initial investment of $5000 in a profitable mutual fund with dividends reinvested and capital gains accepted in shares. By deriving the equation, $y = mx + b$, for A and B, a projection of the future can be made.

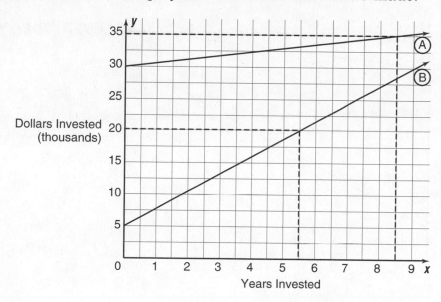

Solve.

1. The y-intercept, b, is the initial investment. Find b for each of the following.

   a. line A **b.** line B

2. The slope of the line, m, is the rate of return. Find m for each of the following.

   a. line A **b.** line B

3. What are the equations of each of the following lines?

   a. line A **b.** line B

Answer each of the following, assuming that the growth of each investment continues in the same pattern.

4. What will be value of the mutual fund after the 11th year?

5. What will be the value of the bank account after the 11th year?

6. When will the mutual fund and the bank account be of equal value?

7. In the long term, which investment has the greater payoff?

13-3 Enrichment

Investments

The graph below represents two different investments. Line A represents an initial investment of $30,000 at a bank paying passbook-savings interest. Line B represents an initial investment of $5000 in a profitable mutual fund with dividends reinvested and capital gains accepted in shares. By deriving the equation, $y = mx + b$, for A and B, a projection of the future can be made.

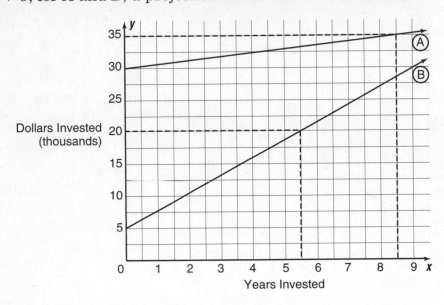

Solve.

1. The y-intercept, b, is the initial investment. Find b for each of the following.

   a. line A **30,000**

   b. line B **5000**

2. The slope of the line, m, is the rate of return. Find m for each of the following.

   a. line A $\dfrac{35,000 - 30,000}{8.5 - 0} \approx$ **588**

   b. line B $\dfrac{20,000 - 5,000}{5.5 - 0} \approx$ **2727**

3. What are the equations of each of the following lines?

   a. line A $y = 588x + 30,000$

   b. line B $y = 2727x + 5000$

Answer each of the following, assuming that the growth of each investment continues in the same pattern.

4. What will be value of the mutual fund after the 11th year?
   $y = 2727(11) + 5000 = \$34,997$

5. What will be the value of the bank account after the 11th year?
   $y = 588(11) + 30,000 = \$36,468$

6. When will the mutual fund and the bank account be of equal value?
   $588x + 30,000 = 2727x + 5000$ $x \approx$ **11.7 years**

7. In the long term, which investment has the greater payoff? **mutual fund**

 Algebra: Concepts and Applications

13-4

Enrichment

Arithmetic Series

An **arithmetic series** is a series in which each term after the first may be found by adding the same number to the preceding term. Let S stand for the following series in which each term is 3 more than the preceding one.

$$S = 2 + 5 + 8 + 11 + 14 + 17 + 20$$

The series remains the same if we reverse the order of all the terms. So let us reverse the order of the terms and add one series to the other, term by term. This is shown at the right.

$$S = \;\; 2 + \;\; 5 + \;\; 8 + 11 + 14 + 17 + 20$$
$$S = 20 + 17 + 14 + 11 + \;\; 8 + \;\; 5 + \;\; 2$$
$$2S = 22 + 22 + 22 + 22 + 22 + 22 + 22$$
$$2S = 7(22)$$

$$S = \frac{7(22)}{2} = 7(11) = 77$$

Let a represent the first term of the series.
Let l represent the last term of the series.
Let n represent the number of terms in the series.
In the preceding example, $a = 2$, $l = 20$, and $n = 7$. Notice that when you add the two series, term by term, the sum of each pair of terms is 22. That sum can be found by adding the first and last terms, $2 + 20$ or $a + l$. Notice also that there are 7, or n, such sums. Therefore, the value of $2S$ is $7(22)$, or $n(a + l)$ in the general case. Since this is twice the sum of the series, you can use the following formula to find the sum of any arithmetic series.

$$S = \frac{n(a + l)}{2}$$

Example 1: Find the sum: $1 + 2 + 3 + 4 + 5 + 6 + 7 + 8 + 9$

$a = 1$, $l = 9$, $n = 9$, so $S = \dfrac{9(1 + 9)}{2} = \dfrac{9 \cdot 10}{2} = 45$

Example 2: Find the sum: $-9 + (-5) + (-1) + 3 + 7 + 11 + 15$

$a = -9$, $l = 15$, $n = 7$, so $S = \dfrac{7(-9 + 15)}{2} = \dfrac{7 \cdot 6}{2} = 21$

Find the sum of each arithmetic series.

1. $3 + 6 + 9 + 12 + 15 + 18 + 21 + 24$

2. $10 + 15 + 20 + 25 + 30 + 35 + 40 + 45 + 50$

3. $-21 + (-16) + (-11) + (-6) + (-1) + 4 + 9 + 14$

4. even whole numbers from 2 through 100

5. odd whole numbers between 0 and 100

Algebra: Concepts and Applications

13-4

Enrichment

Arithmetic Series

An **arithmetic series** is a series in which each term after the first may be found by adding the same number to the preceding term. Let S stand for the following series in which each term is 3 more than the preceding one.

$S = 2 + 5 + 8 + 11 + 14 + 17 + 20$

The series remains the same if we reverse the order of all the terms. So let us reverse the order of the terms and add one series to the other, term by term. This is shown at the right.

$$S = 2 + 5 + 8 + 11 + 14 + 17 + 20$$
$$S = 20 + 17 + 14 + 11 + 8 + 5 + 2$$
$$2S = 22 + 22 + 22 + 22 + 22 + 22 + 22$$
$$2S = 7(22)$$

$$S = \frac{7(22)}{2} = 7(11) = 77$$

Let a represent the first term of the series.
Let l represent the last term of the series.
Let n represent the number of terms in the series.
In the preceding example, $a = 2$, $l = 20$, and $n = 7$. Notice that when you add the two series, term by term, the sum of each pair of terms is 22. That sum can be found by adding the first and last terms, $2 + 20$ or $a + l$. Notice also that there are 7, or n, such sums. Therefore, the value of $2S$ is $7(22)$, or $n(a + l)$ in the general case. Since this is twice the sum of the series, you can use the following formula to find the sum of any arithmetic series.

$$S = \frac{n(a + l)}{2}$$

Example 1: Find the sum: $1 + 2 + 3 + 4 + 5 + 6 + 7 + 8 + 9$

$a = 1$, $l = 9$, $n = 9$, so $S = \frac{9(1 + 9)}{2} = \frac{9 \cdot 10}{2} = 45$

Example 2: Find the sum: $-9 + (-5) + (-1) + 3 + 7 + 11 + 15$

$a = -9$, $l = 15$, $n = 7$, so $S = \frac{7(-9 + 15)}{2} = \frac{7 \cdot 6}{2} = 21$

Find the sum of each arithmetic series.

1. $3 + 6 + 9 + 12 + 15 + 18 + 21 + 24$ **108**

2. $10 + 15 + 20 + 25 + 30 + 35 + 40 + 45 + 50$ **270**

3. $-21 + (-16) + (-11) + (-6) + (-1) + 4 + 9 + 14$ **−28**

4. even whole numbers from 2 through 100 **2550**

5. odd whole numbers between 0 and 100 **2500**

Algebra: Concepts and Applications

13-5

Enrichment

Parabolas Through Three Given Points

If you know two points on a straight line, you can find the equation of the line. To find the equation of a parabola, you need three points on the curve.

For example, here is how to approximate an equation of the parabola through the points $(0, -2)$, $(3, 0)$, and $(5, 2)$.

Use the general equation $y = ax^2 + bx + c$. By substituting the given values for x and y, you get three equations.

$(0, -2)$: $-2 = c$
$(3, 0)$: $0 = 9a + 3b + c$
$(5, 2)$: $2 = 25a + 5b + c$

First, substitute -2 for c in the second and third equations. Then solve those two equations as you would any system of two equations. Multiply the second equation by 5 and the third equation by -3.

$$\begin{array}{rl} 0 = & 45a + 15b - 10 \\ -6 = & -75a - 15b + 6 \\ \hline -6 = & -30a - 15b - 4 \\ a = & \dfrac{1}{15} \end{array}$$

To find b, substitute $\dfrac{1}{15}$ for a in either the second or third equation.

$$0 = 9\left(\frac{1}{15}\right) + 3b - 2$$

$$b = \frac{7}{15}$$

The equation of a parabola through the three points is
$$y = \frac{1}{15}x^2 + \frac{7}{15}x - 2.$$

Find the equation of a parabola through each set of three points.

1. $(1, 5)$, $(0, 6)$, $(2, 3)$

2. $(-5, 0)$, $(0, 0)$, $(8, 100)$

3. $(4, -4)$, $(0, 1)$, $(3, -2)$

4. $(1, 3)$, $(6, 0)$, $(0, 0)$

5. $(2, 2)$, $(5, -3)$, $(0, -1)$

6. $(0, 4)$, $(4, 0)$, $(-4, 4)$

Parabolas Through Three Given Points

If you know two points on a straight line, you can find the equation of the line. To find the equation of a parabola, you need three points on the curve.

For example, here is how to approximate an equation of the parabola through the points $(0, -2)$, $(3, 0)$, and $(5, 2)$.

Use the general equation $y = ax^2 + bx + c$. By substituting the given values for x and y, you get three equations.

$(0, -2)$: $-2 = c$
$(3, 0)$: $0 = 9a + 3b + c$
$(5, 2)$: $2 = 25a + 5b + c$

First, substitute -2 for c in the second and third equations. Then solve those two equations as you would any system of two equations. Multiply the second equation by 5 and the third equation by -3.

$$0 = 45a + 15b - 10$$
$$\underline{-6 = -75a - 15b + 6}$$
$$-6 = -30a - 4$$
$$a = \frac{1}{15}$$

To find b, substitute $\frac{1}{15}$ for a in either the second or third equation.

$$0 = 9\left(\frac{1}{15}\right) + 3b - 2$$
$$b = \frac{7}{15}$$

The equation of a parabola through the three points is
$y = \frac{1}{15}x^2 + \frac{7}{15}x - 2$.

Find the equation of a parabola through each set of three points.

1. $(1, 5)$, $(0, 6)$, $(2, 3)$
   $$y = -\frac{1}{2}x^2 - \frac{1}{2}x + 6$$

2. $(-5, 0)$, $(0, 0)$, $(8, 100)$
   $$y = \frac{25}{26}x^2 + \frac{125}{26}x$$

3. $(4, -4)$, $(0, 1)$, $(3, -2)$
   $$y = -\frac{1}{4}x^2 - \frac{1}{4}x + 1$$

4. $(1, 3)$, $(6, 0)$, $(0, 0)$
   $$y = -\frac{3}{5}x^2 + \frac{18}{5}x$$

5. $(2, 2)$, $(5, -3)$, $(0, -1)$
   $$y = -\frac{19}{30}x^2 + \frac{83}{30}x - 1$$

6. $(0, 4)$, $(4, 0)$, $(-4, 4)$
   $$y = \frac{1}{8}x^2 - \frac{1}{2}x + 4$$

13-6

Enrichment

Student Edition
Pages 580–585

Mechanical Constructions of Parabolas

A given line and a point determine a parabola. Here is one way to construct the curve.

Use a right triangle ABC (or a stiff piece of rectangular cardboard).

Place one leg of the triangle on the given line d. Fasten one end of a string with length BC at the given point F and the other end to the triangle at point B.

Put the tip of a pencil at point P and keep the string tight.

As you move the triangle along the line d, the point of your pencil will trace a parabola.

Draw the parabola determined by line d and point F.

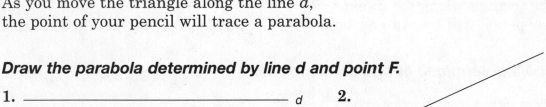

1. _____ d

$F \bullet$

2.

$\bullet$
F

3.

4.

$F \bullet$

d _____

5. Use your drawings to complete this conclusion. The greater the distance of point F from line d,

_____

Enrichment

Student Edition
Pages 580–585

Mechanical Constructions of Parabolas

A given line and a point determine a parabola. Here is one way to construct the curve.

Use a right triangle *ABC* (or a stiff piece of rectangular cardboard).

Place one leg of the triangle on the given line *d*. Fasten one end of a string with length *BC* at the given point *F* and the other end to the triangle at point *B*.

Put the tip of a pencil at point *P* and keep the string tight.

As you move the triangle along the line *d*, the point of your pencil will trace a parabola.

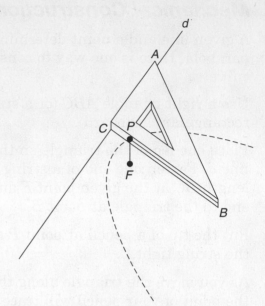

Draw the parabola determined by line d and point F.

1.

2.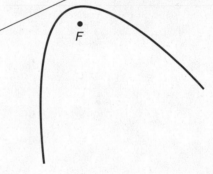

3.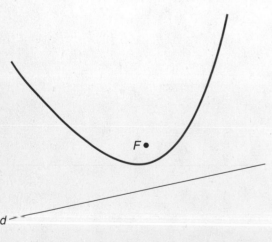

4.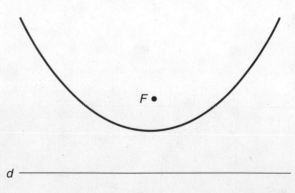

5. Use your drawings to complete this conclusion. The greater the distance of point *F* from line *d*,

the wider the opening of the parabola.

Algebra: Concepts and Applications

Describing Regions

The shaded region inside the triangle can be
described with a system of three inequalities.

$$y < -x + 1$$
$$y > \frac{1}{3}x - 3$$
$$y > -9x - 31$$

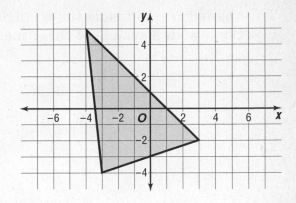

**Write systems of inequalities to describe each region. You may
first need to divide a region into triangles or quadrilaterals.**

1.

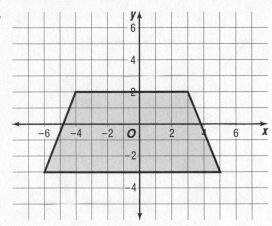

2.

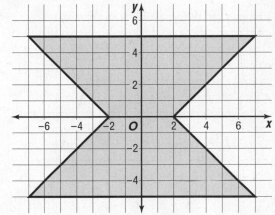

3.

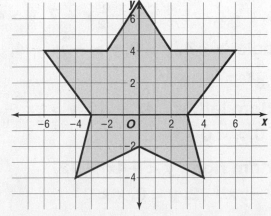

Enrichment

Describing Regions

The shaded region inside the triangle can be described with a system of three inequalities.

$$y < -x + 1$$
$$y > \frac{1}{3}x - 3$$
$$y > -9x - 31$$

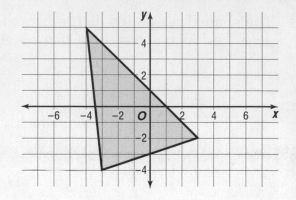

Write systems of inequalities to describe each region. You may first need to divide a region into triangles or quadrilaterals.

1.

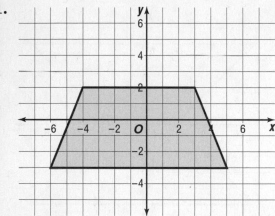

$y < \frac{5}{2}x + 12$

$y < -\frac{5}{2}x + 12$

$y < 2 \qquad y > -3$

2.

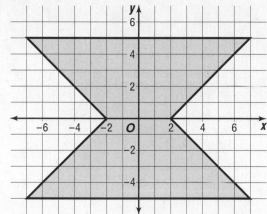

$y > -x - 2 \qquad y < x + 2$
$y > x - 2 \qquad y < -x + 2$
$y < 5 \qquad y > -5$

3.

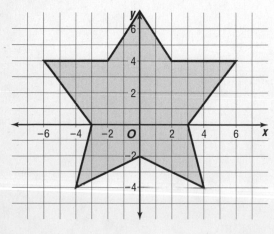

top: $y < \frac{3}{2}x + 7,\ y < -\frac{3}{2}x + 7,\ y > 4$

middle: $y < 4,\ y > 0,\ y > -\frac{4}{3}x - 4,$
$y > \frac{4}{3}x - 4$

bottom left: $y < 4x + 12,\ y > \frac{1}{2}x - 2,$
$y < 0,\ x < 0$

bottom right: $y < -4x + 12,$
$y > -\frac{1}{2}x - 2,\ y < 0,\ x < 0$

14-1

Enrichment

Roots

The symbol $\sqrt{}$ indicates a square root. By placing a number in the upper left, the symbol can be changed to indicate higher roots.

$\sqrt[3]{8} = 2$ because $2^3 = 8$

$\sqrt[4]{81} = 3$ because $3^4 = 81$

$\sqrt[5]{100,000} = 10$ because $10^5 = 100,000$

Find each of the following.

1. $\sqrt[3]{125}$

2. $\sqrt[4]{16}$

3. $\sqrt[8]{1}$

4. $\sqrt[3]{27}$

5. $\sqrt[5]{32}$

6. $\sqrt[3]{64}$

7. $\sqrt[3]{1000}$

8. $\sqrt[3]{216}$

9. $\sqrt[6]{1,000,000}$

10. $\sqrt[3]{1,000,000}$

11. $\sqrt[4]{256}$

12. $\sqrt[3]{729}$

13. $\sqrt[6]{64}$

14. $\sqrt[4]{625}$

15. $\sqrt[5]{243}$

Algebra: Concepts and Applications

Enrichment

Roots

The symbol $\sqrt{}$ indicates a square root. By placing a number in the upper left, the symbol can be changed to indicate higher roots.

$\sqrt[3]{8} = 2$ because $2^3 = 8$

$\sqrt[4]{81} = 3$ because $3^4 = 81$

$\sqrt[5]{100,000} = 10$ because $10^5 = 100,000$

Find each of the following.

1. $\sqrt[3]{125}$ **5**

2. $\sqrt[4]{16}$ **2**

3. $\sqrt[8]{1}$ **1**

4. $\sqrt[3]{27}$ **3**

5. $\sqrt[5]{32}$ **2**

6. $\sqrt[3]{64}$ **4**

7. $\sqrt[3]{1000}$ **10**

8. $\sqrt[3]{216}$ **6**

9. $\sqrt[6]{1,000,000}$ **10**

10. $\sqrt[3]{1,000,000}$ **100**

11. $\sqrt[4]{256}$ **4**

12. $\sqrt[3]{729}$ **9**

13. $\sqrt[6]{64}$ **2**

14. $\sqrt[4]{625}$ **5**

15. $\sqrt[5]{243}$ **3**

Algebra: Concepts and Applications

Lengths on a Grid

You can easily find segment lengths on a grid if the endpoints are grid-line intersections. For horizontal or vertical segments, simply count squares. For diagonal segments, use the Pythagorean Theorem. This theorem states that in any right triangle, if the length of the longest side (the side opposite the right angle) is c and the two shorter sides have lengths a and b, then $c^2 = a^2 + b^2$.

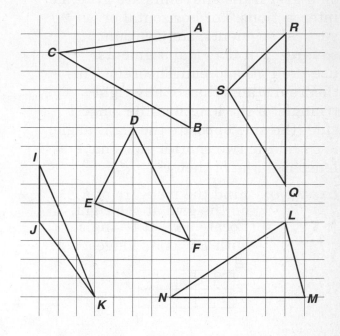

Example: Find the measure of $\overline{EF}$ on the grid at the right. Locate a right triangle with $\overline{EF}$ as its longest side.

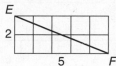

$$EF = \sqrt{2^2 + 5^2}$$
$$= \sqrt{29}$$
$$\approx 5.4 \text{ units}$$

Find each measure to the nearest tenth of a unit.

1. IJ 2. MN 3. RS 4. QS

5. IK 6. JK 7. LM 8. LN

Use the grid above. Find the perimeter of each triangle to the nearest tenth of a unit.

9. $\triangle ABC$ 10. $\triangle QRS$ 11. $\triangle DEF$ 12. $\triangle LMN$

13. Of all the segments shown on the grid, which is longest? What is its length?

14. On the grid, 1 unit = 0.5 cm. How can the answers above be used to find the measures in centimeters?

15. Use your answer from Exercise 8 to calculate the length of segment LN in centimeters. Check by measuring with a centimeter ruler.

16. Use a centimeter ruler to find the perimeter of triangle IJK to the nearest tenth of a centimeter.

Lengths on a Grid

You can easily find segment lengths
on a grid if the endpoints are grid-line
intersections. For horizontal or
vertical segments, simply count
squares. For diagonal segments,
use the Pythagorean Theorem. This
theorem states that in any right
triangle, if the length of the longest
side (the side opposite the right angle)
is c and the two shorter sides have
lengths a and b, then $c^2 = a^2 + b^2$.

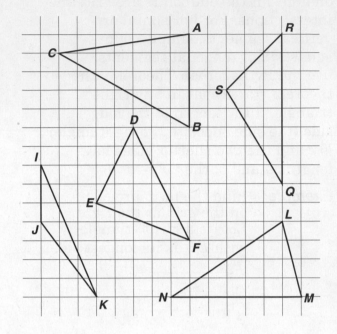

Example: Find the measure of $\overline{EF}$
on the grid at the right.
Locate a right triangle
with $\overline{EF}$ as its longest side.

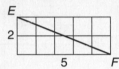

$$EF = \sqrt{2^2 + 5^2}$$
$$= \sqrt{29}$$
$$\approx 5.4 \text{ units}$$

Find each measure to the nearest tenth of a unit.

1. IJ **3**
2. MN **7**
3. RS **4.2**
4. QS **5.8**

5. IK **7.6**
6. JK **5**
7. LM **4.1**
8. LN **7.2**

**Use the grid above. Find the perimeter of each triangle to the
nearest tenth of a unit.**

9. $\triangle ABC$ **20.2**
10. $\triangle QRS$ **18**
11. $\triangle DEF$ **16.6**
12. $\triangle LMN$ **18.3**
**Answers shown are found by rounding segment lengths before
adding.**

13. Of all the segments shown on the
grid, which is longest? What is its
length? **BC = 8.1**

14. On the grid, 1 unit = 0.5 cm. How
can the answers above be used to
find the measures in centimeters?
Divide by 2 or multiply by 0.5.

15. Use your answer from Exercise 8 to
calculate the length of segment LN
in centimeters. Check by measuring
with a centimeter ruler. **3.6 cm**

16. Use a centimeter ruler to find the
perimeter of triangle IJK to the
nearest tenth of a centimeter.
7.8 cm

The Wheel of Theodorus

The Greek mathematicians were intrigued by
problems of representing different numbers and
expressions using geometric constructions.

Theodorus, a Greek philosopher who lived about 425
B.C., is said to have discovered a way to construct the
sequence $\sqrt{1}, \sqrt{2}, \sqrt{3}, \sqrt{4}, \cdots$.

The beginning of his construction is shown. You
start with an isosceles right triangle with sides
1 unit long.

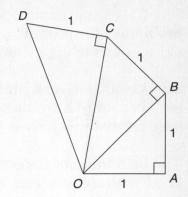

**Use the figure above. Write each length as a radical
expression in simplest form.**

1. line segment AO

2. line segment BO

3. line segment CO

4. line segment DO

5. Describe how each new triangle is added to the figure.

6. The length of the hypotenuse of the first triangle is $\sqrt{2}$. For
the second triangle, the length is $\sqrt{3}$. Write an expression
for the length of the hypotenuse of the nth triangle.

7. Show that the method of construction will always produce
the next number in the sequence. (*Hint:* Find an expression
for the hypotenuse of the $(n + 1)$th triangle.)

8. In the space below, construct a Wheel of Theodorus. Start
with a line segment 1 centimeter long. When does the Wheel
start to overlap?

Enrichment

The Wheel of Theodorus

The Greek mathematicians were intrigued by problems of representing different numbers and expressions using geometric constructions.

Theodorus, a Greek philosopher who lived about 425 B.C., is said to have discovered a way to construct the sequence $\sqrt{1}$, $\sqrt{2}$, $\sqrt{3}$, $\sqrt{4}$, $\cdots$.

The beginning of his construction is shown. You start with an isosceles right triangle with sides 1 unit long.

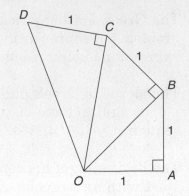

Use the figure above. Write each length as a radical expression in simplest form.

1. line segment *AO* $\sqrt{1}$

2. line segment *BO* $\sqrt{2}$

3. line segment *CO* $\sqrt{3}$

4. line segment *DO* $\sqrt{4}$

5. Describe how each new triangle is added to the figure.
   Draw a new side of length 1 at right angles to the last hypotenuse. Then draw the new hypotenuse.

6. The length of the hypotenuse of the first triangle is $\sqrt{2}$. For the second triangle, the length is $\sqrt{3}$. Write an expression for the length of the hypotenuse of the *n*th triangle.
   $\sqrt{n+1}$

7. Show that the method of construction will always produce the next number in the sequence. (*Hint:* Find an expression for the hypotenuse of the (*n* + 1)th triangle.)
   $\sqrt{(\sqrt{n})^2 + (1)^2} = \sqrt{n+1}$

8. In the space below, construct a Wheel of Theodorus. Start with a line segment 1 centimeter long. When does the Wheel start to overlap? ____
   after length $\sqrt{18}$

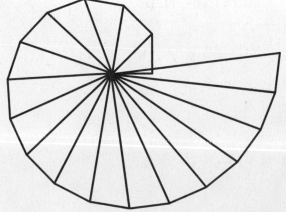

14-4

Enrichment

Student Edition
Pages 620–623

Other Kinds of Means

There are many different kinds of means besides the arithmetic mean. A mean for a set of numbers has these two properties:

a. It typifies or represents the set.

b. It is not less than the least number and it is not greater than the greatest number.

Here are the formulas for the arithmetic mean and three other means.

Arithmetic Mean
Add the numbers in the set. Then divide the sum by n, the number of elements in the set.

$$\frac{x_1 + x_2 + x_3 + \cdots + x_n}{n}$$

Geometric Mean
Multiply all the numbers in the set. Then find the nth root of their product.

$$\sqrt[n]{x_1 \cdot x_2 \cdot x_3 \cdot \cdots \cdot x_n}$$

Harmonic Mean
Divide the number of elements in the set by the sum of the reciprocals of the numbers.

$$\frac{n}{\dfrac{1}{x_1} + \dfrac{1}{x_2} + \dfrac{1}{x_3} + \cdots + \dfrac{1}{x_n}}$$

Quadratic Mean
Add the squares of the numbers. Divide their sum by the number in the set. Then, take the square root.

$$\sqrt{\frac{x_1^2 + x_2^2 + x_3^2 + \cdots + x_n^2}{n}}$$

Find the four different means for each set of numbers.

1. 10, 100

2. 50, 60

3. 1, 2, 3, 4, 5,

4. 2, 2, 4, 4

5. Use the results from Exercises 1 to 4 to compare the relative sizes of the four types of means.

Other Kinds of Means

There are many different kinds of means besides the arithmetic mean. A mean for a set of numbers has these two properties:

a. It typifies or represents the set.

b. It is not less than the least number and it is not greater than the greatest number.

Here are the formulas for the arithmetic mean and three other means.

Arithmetic Mean
Add the numbers in the set. Then divide the sum by n, the number of elements in the set.

$$\frac{x_1 + x_2 + x_3 + \cdots + x_n}{n}$$

Geometric Mean
Multiply all the numbers in the set. Then find the nth root of their product.

$$\sqrt[n]{x_1 \cdot x_2 \cdot x_3 \cdot \cdots \cdot x_n}$$

Harmonic Mean
Divide the number of elements in the set by the sum of the reciprocals of the numbers.

$$\frac{n}{\dfrac{1}{x_1} + \dfrac{1}{x_2} + \dfrac{1}{x_3} + \cdots + \dfrac{1}{x_n}}$$

Quadratic Mean
Add the squares of the numbers. Divide their sum by the number in the set. Then, take the square root.

$$\sqrt{\frac{x_1^2 + x_2^2 + x_3^2 + \cdots + x_n^2}{n}}$$

Find the four different means for each set of numbers.

1. 10, 100
  A = 55   **G = 31.62**
  H = 18.18   **Q = 71.06**

2. 50, 60
  A = 55   **G = 54.77**
  H = 54.55   **Q = 55.23**

3. 1, 2, 3, 4, 5,
  A = 3   **G = 2.61**
  H = 2.19   **Q = 3.32**

4. 2, 2, 4, 4
  A = 3   **G = 2.83**
  H = 2.67   **Q = 3.16**

5. Use the results from Exercises 1 to 4 to compare the relative sizes of the four types of means.
  From least to greatest, the means are the harmonic, geometric, arithmetic, and quadratic means.

Using Radical Equations

The circle with center C and radius r represents Earth. If your eye is at point E, the distance to the horizon is x, or the length of tangent segment ED. The segment drawn from C to D forms a right angle with ED. Thus, $\triangle EDC$ is a right triangle. Apply the Pythagorean Theorem.

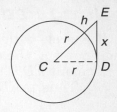

$$(\text{length of } CD)^2 + (\text{length of } ED)^2 = (\text{length of } EC)^2$$
$$r^2 + x^2 = (r + h)^2$$
$$x^2 = (r + h)^2 - r^2$$
$$x = \sqrt{(r + h)^2 - r^2}$$

1. Show that this equation is equivalent to $x = \sqrt{2r + h} \cdot \sqrt{h}$.

If the distance h is very small compared to r, $\sqrt{2r + h}$ is close to $\sqrt{2r}$.
$$x \approx \sqrt{2r} \cdot \sqrt{h}$$
The radius of Earth is about 20,900,000 feet.

$\sqrt{2r} \approx \sqrt{2(20,900,000)} = \sqrt{41,800,000} \approx 6465$ feet. Thus, $x \approx 6465\sqrt{h}$.

If you are h feet above Earth, you are about $6465\sqrt{h}$ feet from the horizon. Since there are 5280 feet in one mile,

$$6465\sqrt{h} \text{ feet} = \frac{5465\sqrt{h}}{5280} \text{ miles} \approx 1.22\sqrt{h} \text{ miles.}$$

Thus, if you are h feet above Earth's surface, you can see $1.22\sqrt{h}$ miles in any direction.

2. How far can you see to the nearest mile if your eye is:
   a. 1454 feet above the ground (the height of the Sears Tower)?
   b. 30,000 feet above the ground (altitude for a commercial airliner)?
   c. $5\frac{1}{2}$ feet from the ground?

A strong wind can severely alter the effect of an actual temperature on the human body. For example, a temperature of 32°F is much more dangerous on a windy day than on a still day. Windchill is a temperature value assigned to a particular combination of wind speed and temperature. If w is the speed of the wind in miles per hour and t is the actual temperature in degrees Fahrenheit, then the approximate windchill temperature in °F is given by the formula

$$\text{windchill temperature} = 92.4 - \frac{(6.91\sqrt{w} + 10.45 - 0.477w)(91.4 - t)}{22.1}.$$

This formula gives reasonably accurate results for the windchill temperature when $5 \le w \le 30$ and $-30 \le t \le 50$.

3. Find the windchill temperature to the nearest degree when the actual temperature is -15°F and the wind speed is
   a. 10 mi/h   b. 20 mi/h   c. 30 mi/h

4. Find the windchill temperature to the nearest degree when the wind speed is 20 mi/h and the actual temperature is
   a. 30°F   b. 0°F   c. -30°F

Algebra: Concepts and Applications

Using Radical Equations

The circle with center C and radius r represents Earth. If your eye is at point E, the distance to the horizon is x, or the length of tangent segment ED. The segment drawn from C to D forms a right angle with ED. Thus, $\triangle EDC$ is a right triangle. Apply the Pythagorean Theorem.

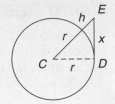

$$(\text{length of } CD)^2 + (\text{length of } ED)^2 = (\text{length of } EC)^2$$
$$r^2 + x^2 = (r + h)^2$$
$$x^2 = (r + h)^2 - r^2$$
$$x = \sqrt{(r + h)^2 - r^2}$$

1. Show that this equation is equivalent to $x = \sqrt{2r + h} \cdot \sqrt{h}$.

$$\sqrt{(r + h)^2 - r^2} = \sqrt{r^2 + 2rh + h^2 - r^2} =$$
$$\sqrt{2rh + h^2} = \sqrt{h(2r + h)} = \sqrt{2r + h} \cdot \sqrt{h}$$

If the distance h is very small compared to r, $\sqrt{2r + h}$ is close to $\sqrt{2r}$.
$$x \approx \sqrt{2r} \cdot \sqrt{h}$$

The radius of Earth is about 20,900,000 feet.

$\sqrt{2r} \approx \sqrt{2(20{,}900{,}000)} = \sqrt{41{,}800{,}000} \approx 6465$ feet. Thus, $x \approx 6465\sqrt{h}$.

If you are h feet above Earth, you are about $6465\sqrt{h}$ feet from the horizon. Since there are 5280 feet in one mile,

$$6465\sqrt{h} \text{ feet} = \frac{5465\sqrt{h}}{5280} \text{ miles} \approx 1.22\sqrt{h} \text{ miles}.$$

Thus, if you are h feet above Earth's surface, you can see $1.22\sqrt{h}$ miles in any direction.

2. How far can you see to the nearest mile if your eye is:

   a. 1454 feet above the ground (the height of the Sears Tower)? **about 47 miles**

   b. 30,000 feet above the ground (altitude for a commercial airliner)? **about 211 miles**

   c. $5\frac{1}{2}$ feet from the ground? **about 2.9 miles**

A strong wind can severely alter the effect of an actual temperature on the human body. For example, a temperature of 32°F is much more dangerous on a windy day than on a still day. Windchill is a temperature value assigned to a particular combination of wind speed and temperature. If w is the speed of the wind in miles per hour and t is the actual temperature in degrees Fahrenheit, then the approximate windchill temperature in °F is given by the formula

$$\text{windchill temperature} = 92.4 - \frac{(6.91\sqrt{w} + 10.45 - 0.477w)(91.4 - t)}{22.1}.$$

This formula gives reasonably accurate results for the windchill temperature when $5 \leq w \leq 30$ and $-30 \leq t \leq 50$.

3. Find the windchill temperature to the nearest degree when the actual temperature is $-15°F$ and the wind speed is
   a. 10 mi/h b. 20 mi/h c. 30 mi/h **−40°F** **−61°F** **−71°F**

4. Find the windchill temperature to the nearest degree when the wind speed is 20 mi/h and the actual temperature is
   a. 30°F   b. 0°F   c. −30°F **4°F** **−39°F** **−82°F**

15-1

Enrichment

Division by Zero?

You may remember being told, "division by zero is not possible" or "division by zero is undefined" or "we never divide by zero." Have you wondered why this is so? Consider the two equations below.

$$\frac{5}{0} = n \qquad \frac{0}{0} = m$$

Because multiplication is the inverse of division, these lead to the following.

$$0 \cdot n = 5 \qquad 0 \cdot m = 0$$

There is no number that will make the first equation true. Any number at all will satisfy the second equation.

For each expression, give the values that must be excluded from the replacement set in order to prevent division by zero.

1. $\dfrac{x + 1}{x - 1}$

2. $\dfrac{2(x + 1)}{2x - 1}$

3. $\dfrac{(x + 1)(x - 1)}{(x + 2)(x - 2)}$

4. $\dfrac{x + y + 3}{(3x - 1)(3y - 1)}$

5. $\dfrac{x^2 + y^2 + z^2}{2xyz}$

6. $\dfrac{(x + y)^2}{x - y}$

Many demonstrations or "proofs" that lead to impossible results include a step involving division by zero. Explain what is wrong with each "proof" below.

7. $0 \cdot 1 = 0$ and $0 \cdot 2 = 0$.

   Therefore, $\dfrac{0}{0} = 1$ and $\dfrac{0}{0} = 2$.

   Therefore, $1 = 2$.

8. Assume that $a = b$.
   Then $ab = a^2$
   Therefore, $ab - b^2 = a^2 - b^2$.
   Next it is shown that $a^2 - b^2 = (a + b)(a - b)$.
   $(a + b)(a - b) = (a + b)\,a - (a + b)b$
   $\qquad\qquad\quad = a^2 + ba - ab - b^2$
   $\qquad\qquad\quad = a^2 + 0 - b^2$
   $\qquad\qquad\quad = a^2 - b^2$
   Therefore, $ab - b^2 = (a + b)(a - b)$.
   Also, $b(a - b) = ba - b^2 = ab - b^2$.
   Therefore, $b(a - b) = (a + b)(a - b)$.
   Therefore, $b = a + b$.
   Therefore, $b = 2b$.
   Therefore, $1 = 2$.

Algebra: Concepts and Applications

Division by Zero?

You may remember being told, "division by zero is not possible"
or "division by zero is undefined" or "we never divide by zero."
Have you wondered why this is so? Consider the two equations
below.

$$\frac{5}{0} = n \qquad \frac{0}{0} = m$$

Because multiplication is the inverse of division, these lead to the following.

$$0 \cdot n = 5 \qquad 0 \cdot m = 0$$

There is no number that will make the first equation true. Any
number at all will satisfy the second equation.

**For each expression, give the values that must be excluded
from the replacement set in order to prevent division by zero.**

1. $\frac{x + 1}{x - 1}$ **x = 1**

2. $\frac{2(x + 1)}{2x - 1}$ **x = $\frac{1}{2}$**

3. $\frac{(x + 1)(x - 1)}{(x + 2)(x - 2)}$ **x = −2 or x = 2**

4. $\frac{x + y + 3}{(3x - 1)(3y - 1)}$ **x = $\frac{1}{3}$, y = $\frac{1}{3}$**

5. $\frac{x^2 + y^2 + z^2}{2xyz}$ **x = 0, y = 0, z = 0**

6. $\frac{(x + y)^2}{x - y}$ **values where x = y**

**Many demonstrations or "proofs" that lead to impossible
results include a step involving division by zero. Explain what
is wrong with each "proof" below.**

7. $0 \cdot 1 = 0$ and $0 \cdot 2 = 0$.

   Therefore, $\frac{0}{0} = 1$ and $\frac{0}{0} = 2$.

   Therefore, $1 = 2$.

   **The second step
   involves division
   by zero.**

8. Assume that $a = b$.
   Then $ab = a^2$
   Therefore, $ab - b^2 = a^2 - b^2$.
   Next it is shown that $a^2 - b^2 = (a + b)(a - b)$.
   $(a + b)(a - b) = (a + b)\, a - (a + b)b$
   $\qquad\qquad = a^2 + ba - ab - b^2$
   $\qquad\qquad = a^2 + 0 - b^2$
   $\qquad\qquad = a^2 - b^2$
   Therefore, $ab - b^2 = (a + b)(a - b)$.
   Also, $b(a - b) = ba - b^2 = ab - b^2$.
   Therefore, $b(a - b) = (a + b)(a - b)$.
   Therefore, $b = a + b$.
   Therefore, $b = 2b$.
   Therefore, $1 = 2$.

   **In moving to the third from the
   last step, each side is divided
   by (a − b). Because a = b,
   that is dividing by zero.**

15-2

Enrichment

Student Edition
Pages 644–649

Complex Fractions

Complex fractions are really not complicated. Remember that a fraction can be interpreted as dividing the numerator by the denominator.

$$\frac{\frac{2}{3}}{\frac{5}{7}} = \frac{2}{3} \div \frac{5}{7} = \frac{2}{3} \cdot \frac{7}{5} = \frac{2(7)}{3(5)} = \frac{14}{15}$$

Let a, b, c, and d be numbers, with $b \neq 0$, $c \neq 0$, and $d \neq 0$.

$$\frac{\frac{a}{b}}{\frac{c}{d}} = \frac{a}{b} \div \frac{c}{d} = \frac{a}{b} \cdot \frac{d}{c} = \frac{ad}{bc}$$

Notice the pattern:

numerator of the answer (ad) $\quad \left[\begin{array}{c} \frac{a}{b} \\ \frac{c}{d} \end{array}\right] \quad$ denominator of the answer (bc)

Example 1: Simplify $\dfrac{\frac{5x}{4}}{\frac{x+2}{3}}$.

$$\frac{\frac{5x}{4}}{\frac{x+2}{3}} = \frac{5x(3)}{4(x+2)}$$

$$= \frac{15x}{4x+8}$$

Example 2: Simplify $\dfrac{\frac{x}{2}+4}{3x-2}$.

$$\frac{\frac{x}{2}+4}{3x-2} = \frac{\frac{x+8}{2}}{\frac{3x-2}{1}}$$

$$= \frac{(x+8)(1)}{2(3x-2)} = \frac{x+8}{6x-4}$$

Simplify each complex fraction.

1. $\dfrac{\frac{2x}{5}}{\frac{y}{6}}$

2. $\dfrac{\frac{4}{5x}}{\frac{3}{x}}$

3. $\dfrac{x-3}{\frac{2x+1}{4}}$

4. $\dfrac{x^2 + \frac{1}{3}}{4x + \frac{1}{3}}$

5. $\dfrac{1 - x^{-1}}{\frac{2x}{5} - 1}$

6. $\dfrac{x + 2x^{-2}}{2 + \frac{x}{3}}$

7. $\dfrac{x}{x + \dfrac{1}{x + \frac{1}{x}}}$

8. $\dfrac{x+2}{x - 2 + \dfrac{1}{x + 2 + \frac{1}{x}}}$

Enrichment

Complex Fractions

Complex fractions are really not complicated. Remember that a fraction can be interpreted as dividing the numerator by the denominator.

$$\frac{\frac{2}{3}}{\frac{5}{7}} = \frac{2}{3} \div \frac{5}{7} = \frac{2}{3} \cdot \frac{7}{5} = \frac{2(7)}{3(5)} = \frac{14}{15}$$

Let a, b, c, and d be numbers, with $b \neq 0$, $c \neq 0$, and $d \neq 0$.

$$\frac{\frac{a}{b}}{\frac{c}{d}} = \frac{a}{b} \div \frac{c}{d} = \frac{a}{b} \cdot \frac{d}{c} = \frac{ad}{bc}$$

Notice the pattern:

numerator of the answer (ad)
$\left[\begin{array}{c}\frac{a}{b} \\ \frac{c}{d}\end{array}\right]$
denominator of the answer (bc)

Example 1: Simplify $\dfrac{\frac{5x}{4}}{\frac{x+2}{3}}$.

$$\frac{\frac{5x}{4}}{\frac{x+2}{3}} = \frac{5x(3)}{4(x+2)}$$

$$= \frac{15x}{4x+8}$$

Example 2: Simplify $\dfrac{\frac{x}{2}+4}{3x-2}$.

$$\frac{\frac{x}{2}+4}{3x-2} = \frac{\frac{x+8}{2}}{\frac{3x-2}{1}}$$

$$= \frac{(x+8)(1)}{2(3x-2)} = \frac{x+8}{6x-4}$$

Simplify each complex fraction.

1. $\dfrac{\frac{2x}{5}}{\frac{y}{6}}$ **12x** / **5y**

2. $\dfrac{\frac{4}{5x}}{\frac{3}{x}}$ **4** / **15**

3. $\dfrac{x-3}{\frac{2x+1}{4}}$ **4x − 12** / **2x + 1**

4. $\dfrac{x^2+\frac{1}{3}}{4x+\frac{1}{3}}$ **3x² + 1** / **12x + 1**

5. $\dfrac{1-x^{-1}}{\frac{2x}{5}-1}$ **5x − 5** / **2x² − 5x**

6. $\dfrac{x+2x^{-2}}{2+\frac{x}{3}}$ **3(x³ + 2)** / **x³ + 6x²**

7. $\dfrac{x}{x+\frac{1}{x+\frac{1}{x}}}$ **x² + 1** / **x² + 2**

8. $\dfrac{x+2}{x-2+\frac{1}{x+2+\frac{1}{x}}}$ **x³ + 4x² + 5x + 2** / **x³ − 2x − 2**

Algebra: Concepts and Applications

Enrichment

Synthetic Division

You can divide a polynomial such as $3x^3 - 4x^2 - 3x - 2$ by a
binomial such as $x - 3$ by a process called **synthetic division.**
Compare the process with long division in the following
explanation.

Example: Divide $(3x^3 - 4x^2 - 3x - 2)$ by $(x - 3)$ using synthetic division.

1. Show the coefficients of the terms in
   descending order.
2. The divisor is $x - 3$. Since 3 is to be
   subtracted, write 3 in the corner ⌐.
3. Bring down the first coefficient, 3.
4. Multiply. $3 \cdot 3 = 9$
5. Add. $-4 + 9 = 5$
6. Multiply. $3 \cdot 5 = 15$
7. Add. $-3 + 15 = 12$
8. Multiply. $3 \cdot 12 = 36$
9. Add. $-2 + 36 = 34$

$$
\begin{array}{c|rrrr}
 & 3 & -4 & -3 & -2 \\
 &   & 9 & 15 & 36 \\
\hline
3 & 3 & 5 & 12 & 34 \\
\end{array}
$$

$3x^2 + 5x + 12$, remainder 34

Check: Use long division.

$$
\begin{array}{r}
3x^2 + 5x + 12 \\
x - 3 \overline{\smash{)}3x^3 - 4x^2 - 3x - 2} \\
\underline{3x^3 - 9x^2} \\
5x^2 - 3x \\
\underline{5x^2 - 15x} \\
12x - 2 \\
\underline{12x - 36} \\
34
\end{array}
$$

The result is $3x^2 + 5x + 12 + \dfrac{34}{x - 3}$.

Divide by using synthetic division. Check your result using long division.

1. $(x^3 + 6x^2 + 3x + 1) \div (x - 2)$

2. $(x^3 - 3x^2 - 6x - 20) \div (x - 5)$

3. $(2x^3 - 5x + 1) \div (x + 1)$

4. $(3x^3 - 7x^2 + 4) \div (x - 2)$

5. $(x^3 + 2x^2 - x + 4) \div (x + 3)$

6. $(x^3 + 4x^2 - 3x - 11) \div (x - 4)$

Algebra: Concepts and Applications

Synthetic Division

You can divide a polynomial such as $3x^3 - 4x^2 - 3x - 2$ by a
binomial such as $x - 3$ by a process called **synthetic division**.
Compare the process with long division in the following
explanation.

Example: Divide $(3x^3 - 4x^2 - 3x - 2)$ by $(x - 3)$ using synthetic division.

1. Show the coefficients of the terms in descending order.
2. The divisor is $x - 3$. Since 3 is to be subtracted, write 3 in the corner ⌐.
3. Bring down the first coefficient, 3.
4. Multiply. $\qquad 3 \cdot 3 = 9$
5. Add. $\qquad -4 + 9 = 5$
6. Multiply. $\qquad 3 \cdot 5 = 15$
7. Add. $\qquad -3 + 15 = 12$
8. Multiply. $\qquad 3 \cdot 12 = 36$
9. Add. $\qquad -2 + 36 = 34$

$$
\begin{array}{c|rrrr}
 & 3 & -4 & -3 & -2 \\
 & & 9 & 15 & 36 \\
\hline
3 & 3 & 5 & 12 & 34 \\
\end{array}
$$

$3x^2 + 5x + 12$, remainder 34

Check: Use long division.

$$
\begin{array}{r}
3x^2 + 5x + 12 \\
x - 3 \overline{\smash{\big)}\ 3x^3 - 4x^2 - 3x - 2} \\
\underline{3x^3 - 9x^2} \\
5x^2 - 3x \\
\underline{5x^2 - 15x} \\
12x - 2 \\
\underline{12x - 36} \\
34
\end{array}
$$

The result is $3x^2 + 5x + 12 + \dfrac{34}{x - 3}$.

Divide by using synthetic division. Check your result using long division.

1. $(x^3 + 6x^2 + 3x + 1) \div (x - 2)$
$x^2 + 8x + 19 + \dfrac{39}{x - 2}$

2. $(x^3 - 3x^2 - 6x - 20) \div (x - 5)$
$x^2 + 2x + 4$

3. $(2x^3 - 5x + 1) \div (x + 1)$
$2x^2 - 2x - 3 + \dfrac{4}{x + 1}$

4. $(3x^3 - 7x^2 + 4) \div (x - 2)$
$3x^2 - x - 2$

5. $(x^3 + 2x^2 - x + 4) \div (x + 3)$
$x^2 - x + 2 - \dfrac{2}{x + 3}$

6. $(x^3 + 4x^2 - 3x - 11) \div (x - 4)$
$x^2 + 8x + 29 + \dfrac{105}{x - 4}$

Sum and Difference of Any Two Like Powers

The sum of any two like powers can be written $a^n + b^n$, where n is a positive integer. The difference of like powers is $a^n - b^n$. Under what conditions are these expressions exactly divisible by $(a + b)$ or $(a - b)$? The answer depends on whether n is an odd or even number.

Use long division to find the following quotients. (HINT: Write $a^3 + b^3$ as $a^3 + 0a^2 + 0a + b^3$.) Is the numerator exactly divisible by the denominator? Write yes or no.

1. $\dfrac{a^3 + b^3}{a + b}$

2. $\dfrac{a^3 + b^3}{a - b}$

3. $\dfrac{a^3 - b^3}{a + b}$

4. $\dfrac{a^3 - b^3}{a - b}$

5. $\dfrac{a^4 + b^4}{a + b}$

6. $\dfrac{a^4 + b^4}{a - b}$

7. $\dfrac{a^4 - b^4}{a + b}$

8. $\dfrac{a^4 - b^4}{a - b}$

9. $\dfrac{a^5 + b^5}{a + b}$

10. $\dfrac{a^5 + b^5}{a - b}$

11. $\dfrac{a^5 - b^5}{a + b}$

12. $\dfrac{a^5 - b^5}{a - b}$

13. Use the words *odd* and *even* to complete these two statements.

    a. $a^n + b^n$ is divisible by $a + b$ if n is _____, and by neither
       $a + b$ nor $a - b$ if n is _____.

    b. $a^n - b^n$ is divisible by $a - b$ if n is _____, and by both
       $a + b$ and $a - b$ if n is _____.

14. Describe the signs of the terms of the quotients when the divisor is $a - b$.

15. Describe the signs of the terms of the quotient when the divisor is $a + b$.

Sum and Difference of Any Two Like Powers

The sum of any two like powers can be written $a^n + b^n$, where n is a positive integer. The difference of like powers is $a^n - b^n$. Under what conditions are these expressions exactly divisible by $(a + b)$ or $(a - b)$? The answer depends on whether n is an odd or even number.

Use long division to find the following quotients. (HINT: Write $a^3 + b^3$ as $a^3 + 0a^2 + 0a + b^3$.) **Is the numerator exactly divisible by the denominator? Write yes or no.**

1. $\dfrac{a^3 + b^3}{a + b}$
   yes

2. $\dfrac{a^3 + b^3}{a - b}$
   no

3. $\dfrac{a^3 - b^3}{a + b}$
   no

4. $\dfrac{a^3 - b^3}{a - b}$
   yes

5. $\dfrac{a^4 + b^4}{a + b}$
   no

6. $\dfrac{a^4 + b^4}{a - b}$
   no

7. $\dfrac{a^4 - b^4}{a + b}$
   yes

8. $\dfrac{a^4 - b^4}{a - b}$
   yes

9. $\dfrac{a^5 + b^5}{a + b}$
   yes

10. $\dfrac{a^5 + b^5}{a - b}$
    no

11. $\dfrac{a^5 - b^5}{a + b}$
    no

12. $\dfrac{a^5 - b^5}{a - b}$
    yes

13. Use the words *odd* and *even* to complete these two statements.

    a. $a^n + b^n$ is divisible by $a + b$ if n is ___**odd**___, and by neither $a + b$ nor $a - b$ if n is ___**even**___.

    b. $a^n - b^n$ is divisible by $a - b$ if n is ___**odd**___, and by both $a + b$ and $a - b$ if n is ___**even**___.

14. Describe the signs of the terms of the quotients when the divisor is $a - b$.
    The terms are all positive.

15. Describe the signs of the terms of the quotient when the divisor is $a + b$.
    The terms are alternately positive and negative.

15-5 Enrichment

Student Edition
Pages 662–667

Work Problems and Similar Right Triangles

"The work problem" has been included in algebra textbooks for a very long time. In older books, the people in the problem always seemed to be digging ditches.

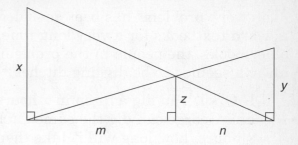

If Olivia can dig a ditch in x hours and George can dig the same ditch in y hours, how long will it take them to dig the ditch if they work together?

You have learned a way to solve this type of problem using rational equations. It can also be solved using a geometric model that uses two overlapping right triangles.

In the drawing, the length x is Olivia's time. The length y is George's time. The answer to the problem is the length of the segment z. The distance $m + n$ can be any convenient length.

Solve each problem.

1. Solve the work problem for $x = 6$ and $y = 3$ by drawing a diagram and measuring.

2. Confirm your solution to problem 1 by writing and solving a rational equation.

3. On a separate sheet of paper, create a word problem to go with the values $x = 6$ and $y = 3$.

4. On a separate sheet of paper, solve this problem with a diagram. Use centimeters and measure to the nearest tenth. Olivia can wash a car in 3 hours. George can wash a car in 4 hours. How long will it take them working together to wash one car?

5. Triangles that have the same shape are called **similar triangles**. You may have learned that corresponding sides of similar triangles form equal ratios. Using the drawing at the top of the page, you can thus conclude that Equations A and B below are true. Use the equations to prove the formula for the work problem.

Equation A

$$\frac{z}{x} = \frac{n}{m + n}$$

Equation B

$$\frac{z}{y} = \frac{m}{m + n}$$

Work Formula

$$\frac{1}{x} + \frac{1}{y} = \frac{1}{z}$$

Work Problems and Similar Right Triangles

"The work problem" has been included in algebra textbooks for a very long time. In older books, the people in the problem always seemed to be digging ditches.

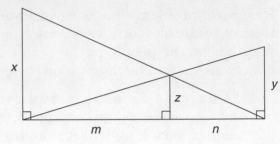

If Olivia can dig a ditch in x hours and George can dig the same ditch in y hours, how long will it take them to dig the ditch if they work together?

You have learned a way to solve this type of problem using rational equations. It can also be solved using a geometric model that uses two overlapping right triangles.

In the drawing, the length x is Olivia's time. The length y is George's time. The answer to the problem is the length of the segment z. The distance $m + n$ can be any convenient length.

**1 h = 0.5 cm
Students' scales
will vary.**

Solve each problem.   **1. z = 2 hours**

1. Solve the work problem for $x = 6$ and $y = 3$ by drawing a diagram and measuring.

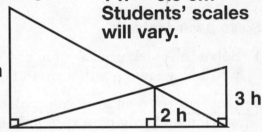

2. Confirm your solution to problem 1 by writing and solving a rational equation.

3. On a separate sheet of paper, create a word problem to go with the values $x = 6$ and $y = 3$. **See students' work.**

2. $\dfrac{t}{6} + \dfrac{t}{3} = 1$ or
$\dfrac{1}{6} + \dfrac{1}{3} = \dfrac{1}{t}$; $t = 2$

4. On a separate sheet of paper, solve this problem with a diagram. Use centimeters and measure to the nearest tenth. Olivia can wash a car in 3 hours. George can wash a car in 4 hours. How long will it take them working together to wash one car? **about 1.7 hours**

5. Triangles that have the same shape are called **similar triangles**. You may have learned that corresponding sides of similar triangles form equal ratios. Using the drawing at the top of the page, you can thus conclude that Equations A and B below are true. Use the equations to prove the formula for the work problem.

Equation A

$\dfrac{z}{x} = \dfrac{n}{m + n}$

Equation B

$\dfrac{z}{y} = \dfrac{m}{m + n}$

Work Formula

$\dfrac{1}{x} + \dfrac{1}{y} = \dfrac{1}{z}$

Adding equations A and B gives $\dfrac{z}{x} + \dfrac{z}{y} = \dfrac{m + n}{m + n}$. **So,** $\dfrac{z}{x} + \dfrac{z}{y} = 1$.

Dividing both sides by z gives $\dfrac{1}{x} + \dfrac{1}{y} = \dfrac{1}{z}$.

Using Rational Expressions and Equations

In 1985 Steve Cram set a world record for the mile run with a
time of 3:46.31. In 1954, Roger Bannister ran the first mile under
4 minutes at 3:59.4. Had they run those times in the same race,
how far in front of Bannister would Cram have been at the finish?

Use $\frac{d}{t} = r$. Since 3 min 46.31 s = 226.31 s, and 3 min 59.4 s = 239.4 s,
Cram's rate was $\frac{5280 \text{ ft}}{226.31 \text{ s}}$ and Bannister's rate was $\frac{5280 \text{ ft}}{239.4 \text{ s}}$.

	r	t	d
Cram	$\frac{5280}{226.31}$	226.31	5280 feet
Bannister	$\frac{5280}{239.4}$	226.31	$\frac{5280}{239.4} \cdot 226.31$ or 4491.3 feet

Therefore, when Cram hit the tape, he would be 5280 − 4491.3, or
288.7 feet, ahead of Bannister. Let's see whether we can develop a
formula for this type of problem.

Let D = the distance raced,
W = the winner's time,
and L = the loser's time.

	r	t	d
Winner	$\frac{D}{W}$	W	$\frac{D}{W} \cdot W = D$
Loser	$\frac{D}{L}$	W	$\frac{D}{L} \cdot W = \frac{DW}{L}$

Following the same pattern, you obtain
the results shown in the table at the right.

The winning distance will be $D - \frac{DW}{L}$.

1. Show that the expression for the winning distance
   is equivalent to $\frac{D(L - W)}{L}$.

**Use the formula winning distance = $\frac{D(L - W)}{L}$ to find the winning
distance for each of the following Olympic races.**

2. women's 400 meter relay: Canada 48.4 s (1928); East Germany
   41.6 s (1980)

3. men's 200 meter freestyle swimming: Mark Spitz 1 min 52.78 s
   (1972); Michael Gross 1 min 47.44 s (1984)

4. men's 50,000 meter walk: Thomas Green 4 h 50 min 10 s
   (1932); Hartwig Gauter 3 h 49 min 24 s (1980)

5. women's 400 meter freestyle relay: Great Britain 5 min 52.8 s
   (1912); East Germany 3 min 42.71 s (1980)

15-6

Enrichment

Using Rational Expressions and Equations

In 1985 Steve Cram set a world record for the mile run with a time of 3:46.31. In 1954, Roger Bannister ran the first mile under 4 minutes at 3:59.4. Had they run those times in the same race, how far in front of Bannister would Cram have been at the finish?

Use $\frac{d}{t} = r$. Since 3 min 46.31 s = 226.31 s, and 3 min 59.4 s = 239.4 s, Cram's rate was $\frac{5280 \text{ ft}}{226.31 \text{ s}}$ and Bannister's rate was $\frac{5280 \text{ ft}}{239.4 \text{ s}}$.

	r	t	d
Cram	$\frac{5280}{226.31}$	226.31	5280 feet
Bannister	$\frac{5280}{239.4}$	226.31	$\frac{5280}{239.4} \cdot 226.31$ or 4491.3 feet

Therefore, when Cram hit the tape, he would be 5280 − 4491.3, or 288.7 feet, ahead of Bannister. Let's see whether we can develop a formula for this type of problem.

Let D = the distance raced,
W = the winner's time,
and L = the loser's time.

Following the same pattern, you obtain the results shown in the table at the right.

	r	t	d
Winner	$\frac{D}{W}$	W	$\frac{D}{W} \cdot W = D$
Loser	$\frac{D}{L}$	W	$\frac{D}{L} \cdot W = \frac{DW}{L}$

The winning distance will be $D - \frac{DW}{L}$.

1. Show that the expression for the winning distance is equivalent to $\frac{D(L - W)}{L}$.

$$D - \frac{DW}{L} = \frac{DL}{L} - \frac{DW}{L}$$
$$= \frac{DL - DW}{L}$$
$$= \frac{D(L - W)}{L}$$

Use the formula winning distance = $\frac{D(L - W)}{L}$ to find the winning distance for each of the following Olympic races.

2. women's 400 meter relay: Canada 48.4 s (1928); East Germany 41.6 s (1980) **56.2 meters**

3. men's 200 meter freestyle swimming: Mark Spitz 1 min 52.78 s (1972); Michael Gross 1 min 47.44 s (1984) **9.5 meters**

4. men's 50,000 meter walk: Thomas Green 4 h 50 min 10 s (1932); Hartwig Gauter 3 h 49 min 24 s (1980) **10,471 meters**

5. women's 400 meter freestyle relay: Great Britain 5 min 52.8 s (1912); East Germany 3 min 42.71 s (1980) **147.5 meters**